CAMBRIDGE LIBRARY COLLECTION

Books of enduring scholarly value

Archaeology

The discovery of material remains from the recent or the ancient past has always been a source of fascination, but the development of archaeology as an academic discipline which interpreted such finds is relatively recent. It was the work of Winckelmann at Pompeii in the 1760s which first revealed the potential of systematic excavation to scholars and the wider public. Pioneering figures of the nineteenth century such as Schliemann, Layard and Petrie transformed archaeology from a search for ancient artifacts, by means as crude as using gunpowder to break into a tomb, to a science which drew from a wide range of disciplines - ancient languages and literature, geology, chemistry, social history - to increase our understanding of human life and society in the remote past.

Patriarchal Palestine

Archibald Henry Sayce (1845–1933) became interested in Middle Eastern languages and scripts while still a teenager. Old Persian and Akkadian cuneiform had recently been deciphered, and popular enthusiasm for these discoveries was running high when Sayce began his academic career at Oxford in 1869. In this 1895 work, he considers the history of the Holy Land in the context of the flood of new documentary and archaeological material which had come to light in the course of the nineteenth century. Sayce's approach opposed the 'higher criticism' which sought to demonstrate that the stories of the Old Testament should not be interpreted literally; in his opinion, 'in the narrative of the Pentateuch we have history and not fiction', and he believed that archaeological discoveries supported his view. Although this approach was already outdated, his reconstruction of the history of the ancient Near East remains of interest to historians of archaeology.

Cambridge University Press has long been a pioneer in the reissuing of out-of-print titles from its own backlist, producing digital reprints of books that are still sought after by scholars and students but could not be reprinted economically using traditional technology. The Cambridge Library Collection extends this activity to a wider range of books which are still of importance to researchers and professionals, either for the source material they contain, or as landmarks in the history of their academic discipline.

Drawing from the world-renowned collections in the Cambridge University Library and other partner libraries, and guided by the advice of experts in each subject area, Cambridge University Press is using state-of-the-art scanning machines in its own Printing House to capture the content of each book selected for inclusion. The files are processed to give a consistently clear, crisp image, and the books finished to the high quality standard for which the Press is recognised around the world. The latest print-on-demand technology ensures that the books will remain available indefinitely, and that orders for single or multiple copies can quickly be supplied.

The Cambridge Library Collection brings back to life books of enduring scholarly value (including out-of-copyright works originally issued by other publishers) across a wide range of disciplines in the humanities and social sciences and in science and technology.

Patriarchal Palestine

*Canaan and the Canaanites
before the Israelitish Conquest*

Archibald Henry Sayce

CAMBRIDGE
UNIVERSITY PRESS

University Printing House, Cambridge, CB2 8BS, United Kingdom

Cambridge University Press is part of the University of Cambridge.
It furthers the University's mission by disseminating knowledge in the pursuit of
education, learning and research at the highest international levels of excellence.

www.cambridge.org
Information on this title: www.cambridge.org/9781108082303

This edition first published 1895
This digitally printed version 2019

ISBN 978-1-108-08230-3 Paperback

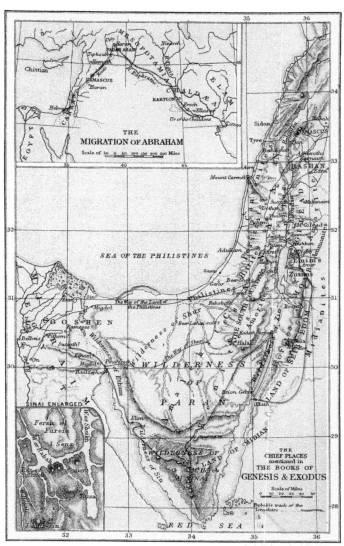

THE
MIGRATION OF ABRAHAM
Scale of 50 0 50 100 150 200 250 Miles

SINAI ENLARGED.

THE
CHIEF PLACES
mentioned in
THE BOOKS OF
GENESIS & EXODUS
Scale of Miles
0 10 20 30 40 50

Stanford's Geographical Establishment.

PATRIARCHAL PALESTINE

BY

THE REV. A. H. SAYCE

PROFESSOR OF ASSYRIOLOGY, OXFORD

WITH A MAP

PUBLISHED UNDER THE DIRECTION OF THE TRACT COMMITTEE

LONDON:
SOCIETY FOR PROMOTING CHRISTIAN KNOWLEDGE,
NORTHUMBERLAND AVENUE, CHARING CROSS, W.C.;
43, QUEEN VICTORIA STREET, E.C.
BRIGHTON: 129, NORTH STREET.
NEW YORK: E. & J. B. YOUNG & CO.
1895.

Richard Clay & Sons, Limited,
London & Bungay.

PREFACE

A FEW years ago the subject-matter of the present volume might have been condensed into a few pages. Beyond what we would gather from the Old Testament, we knew but little about the history and geography of Canaan before the age of its conquest by the Israelites. Thanks, however, to the discovery and decipherment of the ancient monuments of Babylonia and Assyria, of Egypt and of Palestine, all this is now changed. A flood of light has been poured upon the earlier history of the country and its inhabitants, and though we are still only at the beginning of our discoveries we can already sketch the outlines of Canaanitish history, and even fill them in here and there.

Throughout I have assumed that in the narrative of the Pentateuch we have history and not fiction. Indeed the archæologist cannot do otherwise. Monumental research is making it clearer every day that the scepticism of the so-called " higher criticism " is not justified in fact. Those who would examine the proofs of this must turn to my book on *The Higher Criticism and the Verdict of the Monuments.* There I have written purely as an archæologist, who belongs to no theological school, and consequently readers of the work must see in it merely the irreducible minimum of confidence in the historical trustworthiness of the Old Testament, with which oriental archæology can be satisfied. But it is obvious that this irreducible minimum is a good deal less than what a fair-minded historian will admit. The archæological facts support the traditional rather than the so-called " critical " view of the age and authority of the Pentateuch, and tend to show that we have in it not only a historical monument whose statements can be trusted, but also what is substantially a work of the great Hebrew legislator himself.

For those who " profess and call themselves Christians," however, there is another side to the question besides the archæological. The modern " critical " views in regard to the Pentateuch are in violent contradiction to the teaching and belief of the Jewish Church in the time of our Lord, and this teaching and belief has been accepted by Christ and His Apostles, and inherited by the Christian Church. It is a teaching and belief which lies at the root of many of the dogmas of the Church, and if we are to reject or revise it, we must at the same time reject and revise historical Christianity. It is difficult to see how we can call ourselves Christians in the sense which the term has borne for the last eighteen hundred years, and at the same time repudiate or modify, in accordance with our individual fancies, the articles of faith which historical Christianity has maintained everywhere and at all periods. For those who look beyond the covers of grammars and lexicons, the great practical fact of historical Christianity must outweigh all the speculations of individual scholars, however ingenious and elaborate they may be. It is for the individual to harmonize his conclusions with the immemorial doctrine of the Church, not for the Church to reconcile its teaching with the theories of the individual. Christ promised that the Spirit of God should guide His Apostles and their followers into " all truth," and those who believe the promise cannot also believe that the " Spirit of Truth " has been at any time a Spirit of illusion.

Oriental archæology, at all events, is on the side of those who see in the Hebrew patriarchs real men of flesh and blood, and who hold that in the narratives of the Pentateuch we have historical records many of which go back to the age of the events they describe. Each fresh discovery made by the archæologist yields fresh testimony to the truth of the Old Testament stories. Since the manuscript of the present work was ready for the press, two such discoveries have been made by Mr. Pinches, to whom oriental archæology and Biblical research are already under such deep obligations, and it has been possible only to glance at them in the text.

He has found a broken cuneiform tablet which once gave an account of the reign of Khammurabi, the contemporary of Chedor-laomer and Arioch, of the wars that he carried on, and of the steps by which he rose to the supreme power in Babylonia, driving the Elamites out of it, overthrowing his rival Arioch, and making Babylon for the first time the capital of a united kingdom. Unfortunately the tablet is much broken, but what is left alludes to his campaigns against Elam and Rabbatu—perhaps a city of Palestine, of his reduction of Babylon, and of his successes against Eri-Aku or Arioch of Larsa, Tudghulla or Tidal, the son of Gazza . . ., and Kudur-Lagamar or Chedor-laomer himself. The Hebrew text of Genesis has thus been verified even to the spelling of the proper names. The other discovery of Mr. Pinches is still more interesting. The name of Ab-ramu or Abram had already been found in Babylonian contracts of the age of Khammurabi ; Mr. Pinches has now found in them the specifically Hebrew names of Ya'qub-ilu or Jacob-el and Yasup-ilu or Joseph-el. It will be remembered that the names of Jacob-el and Joseph-el had already been detected among the places in Palestine conquered by the Egyptian monarch Thothmes III., and it had been accordingly inferred that the full names of the Hebrew patriarchs must have been Jacob-el and Joseph-el. Jacob and Joseph are abbreviations analogous to Jephthah by the side of Jiphthah-el (Josh. xix. 14), of Jeshurun by the side of Isra-el,

or of the Egyptian Yurahma by the side of the
Biblical Jerahme-el. As is mentioned in a later page,
a discovery recently made by Prof. Flinders Petrie
has shown that the name of Jacob-el was actually
borne not only in Babylonia, but also in the West.
Scarabs exist, which he assigns to the period when
Egypt was ruled by invaders from Asia, and on
which is written the name of a Pharaoh Ya'aqub-
hal or Jacob-el.

Besides the names of Jacob-el and Joseph-el, Mr.
Pinches has met with other distinctively Hebrew
names, like Abdiel, in deeds drawn up in the time
of the dynasty to which Khammurabi belonged.
There were therefore Hebrews—or at least a Hebrew-
speaking population—living in Babylonia at the
period to which the Old Testament assigns the
lifetime of Abraham. But this is not all. As I
pointed out five years ago, the name of
Khammurabi himself, like those of the rest of the
dynasty of which he was a member, are not
Babylonian but South Arabian. The words with
which they are compounded, and the divine names
which they contain, do not belong to the Assyrian
and Babylonian language, and there is a cuneiform
tablet in which they are given with their Assyrian
translations. The dynasty must have had close
relations with South Arabia. This, however, is not
the most interesting part of the matter. The
names are not South Arabian only, they are
Hebrew as well. That of Khammu-rabi, for
instance, is compounded with the name of the god

'Am, which is written 'Ammi in the name of his descendant Ammi-zaduqa, and 'Am or 'Ammi characterizes not only South Arabia, but the Hebrew-speaking lands as well. We need only mention names like Ammi-nadab or Ben-Ammi in illustration of the fact. Equally Hebrew and South Arabian is *zaduqa* or *zadoq;* but it was a word unknown to the Assyrian language of Babylonia.

When Abraham therefore was born in Ur of the Chaldees, a dynasty was ruling there which was not of Babylonian origin, but belonged to a race which was at once Hebrew and South Arabian. The contract tablets prove that a population with similar characteristics was living under them in the country. Could there be a more remarkable confirmation of the statements which we find in the tenth chapter of Genesis ? There we read that " unto Eber were born two sons : the name of the one was Peleg," the ancestor of the Hebrews, while the name of the other was Joktan, the ancestor of the tribes of South Arabia. The parallelism between the Biblical account and the latest discovery of archæological science is thus complete, and makes it impossible to believe that the Biblical narrative would have been compiled in Palestine at the late date to which our modern " critics " would assign it. All recollection of the facts embodied in it would then have long passed away.

Even while I write Prof. Hommel is announcing fresh discoveries which bear on the early history of the Book of Genesis. Cuneiform tablets have turned up from which we gather that centuries before the age of Abraham, a king of Ur, Ine-Sin by name, had not only overrun Elam, but had also conquered Simurru, the Zemar of Gen. x. 18, in the land of Phœnicia. A daughter of the same king or of one of his immediate successors, was high-priestess both of Elam and of Markhas or Mer'ash in Northern Syria, while Kimas or Northern Arabia was overrun by the Babylonian arms. Proofs consequently are multiplying of the intimate relations that existed between Babylonia and Western Asia long before the era of the Patriarchs, and we need no longer feel any surprise that Abraham should have experienced so little diffi-culty in migrating into Canaan, or that he should have found there the same culture as that which he had left behind in Ur. The language and script of Babylonia must have been almost as well known to the educated Canaanite as to himself, and the records of the Patriarchal Age would have been preserved in the libraries of Canaan down to the time of its conquest by the Israelites.

Perhaps a word or two is needed in explanation of the repetitions which will be found here and there in the following pages. They have been necessitated by the form into which I have been obliged to cast the book. A consecutive history of Patriarchal Palestine cannot be written at present, if indeed it ever can be, and the subject therefore has to be treated under a series of separate heads.

This has sometimes made repetitions unavoidable without a sacrifice of clearness.

In conclusion it will be noted, that the name of the people who were associated with the Philistines in their wars against Egypt and occupation of Palestine has been changed from Zakkur to Zakkal. This has been in consequence of a keen-sighted observation of Prof. Hommel. He has pointed out that in a Babylonian text of the Kassite period, the people in question are mentioned under the name of Zaqqalû, which settles the reading of the hieroglyphic word. (See the *Proceedings* of the Society of Biblical Archæology for May 1895.)

A. H. SAYCE.

September 30, 1895.

THE KINGS OF EGYPT AND BABYLONIA DURING THE PATRIARCHAL AGE.

EGYPT.

Dynasties XV., XVI., and XVII.—Hyksos or Shepherd-kings (from Manetho).

Dynasty XV.—

				yrs.	mths.
1.	Salatis	reigned	13	0
2.	Beon, or Bnon ...	,,	44	0
3.	Apakhnas, or Pakhnan	,,	36	7
4.	Apôphis I.	,,	61	0
5.	Yanias or Annas ...	,,	50	1
6.	Assis	,,	49	2

Of the Sixteenth Dynasty nothing is known. Of the Seventeenth the monuments have given us the names of Apôphis II. (Aa-user-Ra) and Apôphis III. (Aa-ab-tani-Ra), in whose reign the war of independence began under the native prince of Thebes, and lasted for four generations.

Dynasty XVIII.—

Manetho.

1. Neb-pehuti-Ra, Ahmes (more than 20 years). — Amosis.
2. Ser-ka-Ra, Amon-hotep I., his son (20 years 7 months.) — Amenophis I.
3. Aa-kheper-ka-Ra, Thothmes I., his son, and queen Amen-sit. — Chebron.
4. Aa-kheper-n-Ra, Thothmes II., his son, and wife Hatshepsu I. (more than 9 years). — Amensis.
5. Khnum-Amon, Hatshepsu II., Mâ-ka-Ra his sister (more than 16 years). — . . .
6. Ra-men-Kheper,Thothmes III.,her brother (57 years, 11 months, 1 day, from March 20, B.C. 1503 to Feb. 14, B.C. 1449). — Misaphris.
7. Aa-khepru-Ra, Amon-hotep II., his son (more than 5 years). — Misphragmutho-sis.
8. Men-khepru-Ra, Thothmes IV., his son (more than 7 years). — Touthmosis.
9. Neb-mâ-Ra, Amon-hotep III., his son (more than 35 years), and queen Teie. — Amenophis II.
10. Nefer-khepru-Ra, Amon-hotep IV., Khu-n-Aten (also called Khuriya), his son (more than 17 years). — Horos.
11. Ankh-khepru-Ra and queen Meri-Aten. — Akherres.
12. Tut-ânkh-Amon Khepru-neb-Ra,and queen Ankh-nes-Amon. — Rathotis.
13. Aten-Ra-nefer-nefru-mer-Aten. — . . .
14. Ai kheper-khepru-ar-mâ-Ra, and queen Thi (more than 4 years). — . . .
15. Hor-m-hib Mi-Amon Ser-khepru-ka (more than 3 years). — Armais.

Dynasty XIX.—

1. Men-pehuti-Ra, Ramessu I. (more than 2   Ramesses.
   years).
2. Men-mâ-Ra, Seti I., Mer-n-Ptah I. (more than   Sethos.
   27 years), his son.
3. User-mâ-Ra, Sotep-n-Ra, Ramessu II., Mi-   . . .
   Amon (B.C. 1348—1281), his son.
4. Mer-n-Ptah II., Hotep-hi-ma Ba-n-Ra, Mi-   Ammenephthes.
   Amon, his son.
5. User-khepru-Ra, Seti II., Mer-n-Ptah III., his   Sethos Ramesses.
   brother.
6. Amon-mesu Hik-An Mer-Khâ-Ra Sotep-n-   Amenemes.
   Ra, usurper.
7. Khu-n-Ra Sotep-n-Ra, Mer-n-Ptah IV., Si-   Thuoris.
   Ptah (more than 6 years), and queen Ta-user.

Dynasty XX.—

1. Set-nekht, Merer-Mi-Amon (recovered the kingdom from the
   Phœnician Arisu).
2. Ramessu III., Hik-An, his son (more than 32 years).
3. Ramessu IV., Hik-Mâ Mi-Amon (more than 11 years).
4. Ramessu V., User-Mâ-s-Kheper-n-Ra Mi-Amon (more than 4 years).
5. Ramessu VI., Neb-mâ-Ra Mi-Amon Amon-hir-khopesh-f (Ramessu
   Meri-Tum, a rival king in Northern Egypt).
6. Ramessu VII., At-Amon User-mâ-Ra Mi-Amon.
7. Ramessu VIII., Set-hir-khopesh-f Mi-Amon User-mâ-Ra Khu-n-
   Amon.
8. Ramessu IX., Si-Ptah S-khâ-n-Ra Mi-Amon (19 years).
9. Ramessu X., Nefer-ka-Ra Mi-Amon Sotep-n-Ra (more than 10
   years).
10. Ramessu XI., Amon-hir-khopesh-f Kheper-mâ-Ra Sotep-n-Ra.
11. Ramessu XII., Men-mâ-Ra Mi-Amon Sotep-n-Ptah Khâ-m-Uas
    (more than 27 years).

Dynasty I. of Babylon—

1. Sumu-abi, 15 years, B.C. 2458.
2. Sumu-la-ilu, his son, 35 years.
3. Zabû, his son, 14 years.
4. Abil-Sin, his son, 18 years.
5. Sin-muballidh, his son, 30 years.
6. Khammu-rabi, his son, 55 years (at first under the sovereignty of Chedor-laomer, the Elamite; by the conquest of Eri-Aku and the Elamites he unites Babylonia, B.C. 2320).
7. Samsu-iluna, his son, 35 years.
8. Ebisum, or Abi-esukh, his son, 25 years.
9. Ammi-satana, his son, 25 years.
10. Ammi-zaduga, his son, 21 years.
11. Samsu-satana, his son, 31 years.

Dynasty II. of Uru-azagga, B.C. 2154—

1. Anman, 51 (or 60) years.
2. Ki-nigas, 55 years.
3. Damki-ili-su, 46 years.
4. Iskipal, 15 years.
5. Sussi, his brother, 27 years.
6. Gul-kisar, 55 years.
7. Kirgal-daramas, his son, 50 years.
8. A-dara-kalama, his son, 28 years.
9. A-kur-du-ana, 26 years.
10. Melamma-kurkura, 6 years.
11. Bel-ga[mil?], 9 years.

Dynasty III., of the Kassites, B.C.
 1786—
 1. Gandis, or Gaddas, 16 years.
 2. Agum-Sipak, his son, 22 years.
 3. Guya-Sipak, his son, 22 years.
 4. Ussi, his son, 8 years.
 5. Adu-medas, ... years.
 6. Tazzi-gurumas, ... years.
 7. Agum-kak-rimi, his son, ... years.
 .   .   .   .   .   ,
 14. Kallimma-Sin.[1]
 15. Kudur-Bel.
 16. Sagarakti-buryas, his son.
 17. Kuri-galzu I.
 18. Kara-indas.
 19. Burna-buryas, his nephew, B.C. 1400.
 20. Kara-Khardas, son of Kara-indas.
 21. Nazi-bugas, or Su-zigas, an usurper.
 22. Kuri-galzu II., son of Burna-buryas, 2 .. years.
 23. Nazi-Maruttas, his son, 26 years.

 24. Kadasman-Turgu, his son, 17 years.
 25. Kadasman-Burias, his son, 2 years.
 26. Gis-amme . . ti, 6 years.
 27. Saga-rakti-suryas 13 years.
 28. Kasbat, or Bibe-yasu, his son, 8 years.
 29. Bel-nadin-sumi, 1 year 6 months.
 30. Kadasman-Kharbe, 1 year 6 months.
 31. Rimmon - nadin - sumi, 6 years.
 32. Rimmon-sum-utsur, 30 years (including 7 years of occupation of Babylon by the Assyrian king, Tiglath-Ninip).
 33. Mile-Sipak, 15 years.
 34. Merodach-baladan I., his son, 13 years.
 35. Zamama-nadin-sumi I., 1 year.
 36. Bel-sum-iddin, 3 years.

[1] The following order of succession is taken from Dr. Hilprecht.

CONTENTS

PATRIARCHAL PALESTINE

CHAPTER I

THE LAND

PATRIARCHAL PALESTINE! There are some who would tell us that the very name is a misnomer. Have we not been assured by the German critics and their English disciples that there were no patriarchs and no Patriarchal Age? And yet, the critics notwithstanding, the Patriarchal Age has actually existed. While criticism, so-called, has been busy in demolishing the records of the Pentateuch, archæology, by the spade of the excavator and the patient skill of the decipherer, has been equally busy in restoring their credit. And the monuments of the past are a more solid argument than the guesses and prepossessions of the modern theorist. The clay tablet and inscribed stone are better witnesses to the truth than literary tact or critical scepticism. That Moses and his contemporaries could neither read nor write may

have been proved to demonstration by the critic ;
yet nevertheless we now know, thanks to archæological discovery, that it would have been a miracle
if the critic were right. The Pentateuch is, after
all, what it professes to be, and the records it
contains are history and not romance.

The question of its authenticity involves issues
more serious and important than those which have
to do merely with history or archæology. We are
sometimes told indeed, in all honesty of purpose,
that it is a question of purely literary interest, without influence on our theological faith. But the whole
fabric of the Jewish Church in the time of our
Lord was based upon the belief that the Law of
Moses came from God, and that this God " is not a
man that He should lie." And the belief of the
Jewish Church was handed on to the Christian
Church along with all its consequences. To revise
that belief is to revise the dogmas of the Christian
Church as they have been held for the last eighteen
centuries ; to reject it utterly is to reject the primary
document of the faith into which we have been
baptized.

It is not, however, with theological matters that
we are now concerned. Patriarchal Palestine is for
us the Palestine of the Patriarchal Age, as it has
been disclosed by archæological research, not the
Palestine in which the revelation of God's will to
man was to be made. It is sufficient for us that
the Patriarchal Age has been shown by modern
discovery to be a fact, and that in the narratives of

the Book of Genesis we have authentic records of the past. There was indeed a Patriarchal Palestine, and the glimpses of it that we get in the Old Testament have been illustrated and supplemented by the ancient monuments of the Oriental world.

Whether the name of Palestine can be applied to the country with strict accuracy at this early period is a different question. Palestine is Philistia, the land of the Philistines, and the introduction of the name was subsequent to the settlement of the Philistines in Canaan and the era of their victories over Israel. As we shall see later on, it is probable that they did not reach the Canaanitish coast until the Patriarchal Age was almost, if not entirely, past. Their name does not occur in the cuneiform correspondence which was carried on between Canaan and Egypt in the century before the Exodus, and they are first heard of as forming part of that great confederacy of northern tribes which attacked Egypt and Canaan in the days of Moses. But, though the term Canaan would doubtless be more correct than Palestine, the latter has become so purely geographical in meaning that we can employ it without reference to history or date. Its signification is too familiar to cause mistakes, and it can therefore be used proleptically, just as the name of the Philistines themselves is used proleptically in the twenty-first chapter of Genesis. Abimelech was king of a people who inhabited the same part of the country as the Philistines in later times, and were thus their earlier representatives.

B

The term "Palestine" then is used geographically without any reference to its historical origin.
It denotes the country which is known as Canaan
in the Old Testament, which was promised to
Abraham and conquered by his descendants.   It is
the land in which David ruled and in which Christ
was born, where the prophets prepared the way
for the Gospel and the Christian Church was
founded.

Shut in between the Desert of Arabia and the
Mediterranean Sea on the east and west, it is a
narrow strip of territory, for the most part mountainous, rugged, and barren. Northward the Lebanon
and Anti-Lebanon come to meet it from Syria, the
Anti-Lebanon culminating in the lofty peaks and
precipitous ravines of Mount Hermon (9383 feet
above the level of the sea), while Lebanon runs
southward till it juts out into the sea in its sacred
headland of Carmel. The fertile plain of Esdraelon
or Megiddo separates the mountains of the north
from those of the south.   These last form a broken
plateau between the Jordan and the Dead Sea on
the one side and the Plain of Sharon and the sea-
coast of the Philistines on the other, until they
finally slope away into the arid desert of the south.
Here, on the borders of the wilderness, was Beer-
sheba the southern limit of the land in the days
of the monarchy, Dan, its northern limit, lying far
away to the north at the foot of Hermon, and not
far from the sources of the Jordan.

Granite and gneiss, overlaid with hard dark sandstone and masses of secondary limestone, form as it were the skeleton of the country. Here and there, at Carmel and Gerizim, patches of the tertiary nummulite of Egypt make their appearance, and in the plains of Megiddo and the coast, as well as in the " Ghor " or valley of the Jordan, there is rich alluvial soil. But elsewhere all is barren or nearly so, cultivation being possible only by terracing the cliffs, and bringing the soil up to them from the plains below with slow and painful labour. It has often been said that Palestine was more widely cultivated in ancient times than it is to-day. But if so, this was only because a larger area of the cultivable ground was tilled. The plains of the coast, which are now given over to malaria and Beduin thieves, were doubtless thickly populated and well sown. But of ground actually fit for cultivation there could not have been a larger amount than there is at present.

It was not in any way a well-wooded land. On the slopes of the Lebanon and of Carmel, it is true, there were forests of cedar-trees, a few of which still survive, and the Assyrian kings more than once speak of cutting them down or using them in their buildings at Nineveh. But south of the Lebanon forest trees were scarce ; the terebinth was so unfamiliar a sight in the landscape as to become an object of worship or a road-side mark. Even the palm grew only on the sea-coast or in the valley of the Jordan, and the tamarisk and sycamore were hardly more than shrubs.

Nevertheless when the Israelites first entered Canaan, it was in truth a land "flowing with milk and honey." Goats abounded on the hills, and the bee of Palestine, though fierce, is still famous for its honey-producing powers. The Perizzites or "fellahin" industriously tilled the fields, and high-walled cities stood on the mountain as well as on the plain.

The highlands, however, were deficient in water. A few streams fall into the sea south of Carmel, but except in the spring, when they have been swollen by the rains, there is but little water in them. The Kishon, which irrigates the plain of Megiddo, is a more important river, but it too is little more than a mountain stream. In fact, the Jordan is the only river in the true sense of the word which Palestine possesses. Rising to the north of the waters of Merom, now called Lake Hûleh, it flows first into the Lake of Tiberias, and then through a long deep valley into the Dead Sea. Here at a depth of 1293 feet below the level of the sea it is swallowed up and lost ; the sea has no outlet, and parts with its stagnant waters through evaporation alone. The evaporation has made it intensely salt, and its shores are consequently for the most part the picture of death.

In the valley of the Jordan, on the other hand, vegetation is as luxuriant and tropical as in the forests of Brazil. Through a dense undergrowth of canes and shrubs the river forces its way, rushing forward towards its final gulf of extinc-

tion with a fall of 670 feet since it left the Lake
of Tiberias. But the distance thus travelled by it
is long in comparison with its earlier fall of 625
feet between Lake Hûleh and the Sea of Galilee.
Here it has cut its way through a deep gorge,
the cliffs of which rise up almost sheer on either
side.

The Jordan has taken its name from its rapid
fall. The word comes from a root which signifies
"to descend," and the name itself means "the
down-flowing." We can trace it back to the
Egyptian monuments of the nineteenth and twentieth dynasties. Ramses II., the Pharaoh of the
Oppression, has inscribed it on the walls of Karnak,
and Ramses III., who must have reigned while the
Israelites were still in the wilderness, enumerates
the "Yordan" at Medînet Habu among his conquests
in Palestine. In both cases it is associated with
"the Lake of Rethpana," which must accordingly
be the Egyptian name of the Dead Sea. Rethpana
might correspond with a Hebrew Reshphôn, a
derivative from Resheph, the god of fire. Canaanite
mythology makes the sparks his "children" (Job v.
7) and it may be, therefore, that in this old name
of the Dead Sea we have a reference to the overthrow of the cities of the plain.

Eastward of the Dead Sea and the Jordan the
country is again mountainous and bare. Here
were the territories of Reuben and Gad, and the
half-tribe of Manasseh; here also were the kingdoms of Moab and Ammon, of Bashan and the

Amorites.   Here too was the land of Gilead, south of the Lake of Tiberias and north of the Dead Sea.

We can read the name of Muab or Moab on the base of the second of the six colossal statues which Ramses II. erected in front of the northern pylon of the temple of Luxor.   It is there included among his conquests.   The statue is the only Egyptian monument on which the name has hitherto been found.   But this single mention is sufficient to guarantee its antiquity, and to prove that in the days before the Exodus it was already well known in Egypt.

To the north of Moab came the kingdom of Ammon, or the children of Ammi.   The name of Ammon was a derivative from that of the god Ammi or Ammo, who seems to have been regarded as the ancestor of the nation, and " the father of the children of Ammon " was accordingly called Ben-Ammi, " the son of Ammi " (Gen. xix. 38).   Far away in the north, close to the junction of the rivers Euphrates and Sajur, and but a few miles to the south of the Hittite stronghold of Carchemish, the worship of the same god seems to have been known to the Aramæan tribes.   It was here that Pethor stood, according to the Assyrian inscriptions, and it was from Pethor that the seer Balaam came to Moab to curse the children of Israel.   Pethor, we are told, was " by the river (Euphrates) of the land of the children of Ammo," where the word represents a proper name (Num.

xxii. 5). To translate it "his people," as is done by the Authorized Version, makes no sense. On the Assyrian monuments Ammon is sometimes spoken of as Beth-Ammon, "the house of Ammon," as if Ammon had been a living man.

Like Moab, Ammon was a region of limestone mountains and barren cliffs. But there were fertile fields on the banks of the Jabbok, the sources of which rose not far from the capital Rabbath.

North of Gilead and the Yarmuk was the volcanic plateau of Bashan, Ziri-Basana, or "the Plain of Bashan," as it is termed in the cuneiform tablets of Tel el-Amarna. Its western slope towards the Lakes of Merom and Tiberias was known as Golan (now Jolân); its eastern plateau of metallic lava was Argob, "the stony" (now El Lejja). Bashan was included in the Haurân, the name of which we first meet with on the monuments of the Assyrian king Assur-bani-pal. To the north it was bounded by Ituræa, so named from Jetur, the son of Ishmael (Gen. xxv. 15), the road through Ituræa (the modern Jedur) leading to Damascus and its well-watered plain.

The gardens of Damascus lie 2260 feet above the sea. In the summer the air is cooled by the mountain breezes; in the winter the snow sometimes lies upon the surface of the land. Westward the view is closed by the white peaks of Anti-Lebanon and Hermon; eastward the eye wanders over a green plain covered with the mounds of old towns and villages, and intersected by the clear and rapid streams of the Abana and Pharphar. But the Abana has now become the Barada, or "cold one," while the Pharphar is the Nahr el-Awaj.

The Damascus of to-day stands on the site of the city from which St. Paul escaped, and "the street which is called Straight" can still be traced by its line of Roman columns. But it is doubtful whether the Damascus of the New Testament and of to-day is the same as the Damascus of the Old Testament. Where the walls of the city have been exposed to view, we see that their Greek foundations rest on the virgin soil; no remains of an earlier period lie beneath them. It may be, therefore, that the Damascus of Ben-Hadad and Hazael is marked rather by one of the mounds in the plain than by the modern town. In one of these the stone statue of a man, in the Assyrian style, was discovered a few years ago.

An ancient road leads from the peach-orchards of Damascus, along the banks of the Abana and over Anti-Lebanon, to the ruins of the temple of the Sun-god at Baalbek. The temple as we see it is of the age of the Antonines, but it occupies the place of one which stood in Heliopolis, the city of the Sun-god, from immemorial antiquity. Relics of an older epoch still exist in the blocks of stone of colossal size which serve as the foundation of the western wall. Their bevelling reminds us of Phœnician work.

Baalbek was the sacred city of the Bek'a, or "cleft" formed between Lebanon and Anti-Lebanon by the gorge through which the river Litâny rushes down to the sea. Once and once only is it referred to in the Old Testament. Amos (i. 5) declares that the Lord " will break the bar of Damascus and cut off the inhabitant from Bikath-On "—the Bek'a of On. The name of On reminds us that the Heliopolis of Egypt, the city of the Egyptian Sun-god, was also called On, and the question arises whether the name and worship of the On of Syria were not derived from the On of Egypt. For nearly two centuries Syria was an Egyptian province, and the priests of On in Egypt may well have established themselves in the " cleft " valley of Cœle-Syria.

From Baalbek, the city of " Baal of the Bek'a," the traveller makes his way across Lebanon, and under the snows of Jebel Sannîn—nearly 9000 feet in height—to the old Phœnician city of Beyrout. Beyrout is already mentioned in the cuneiform tablets of Tel el-Amarna under the name of Beruta or Beruna, " the cisterns." It was already a seaport of Phœnicia, and a halting-place on the high road that ran along the coast.

The coastland was known to the Greeks and Romans as Phœnicia, " the land of the palm." But its own inhabitants called it Canaan, " the lowlands." It included not only the fringe of cultivated land by the sea-shore, but the western slopes of the Lebanon as well. Phœnician colonies and outposts had been planted inland, far away from the coast, as at Laish, the future Dan, where "the people dwelt careless," though "they were far away from the Sidonians," or at Zemar (the modern Sumra) and Arka (still called by the same name). The territory of the Phœnicians stretched southward as far as Dor (now Tantûrah), where it met the advance guard of the Philistines.

Such was Palestine, the promised home of Israel. It was a land of rugged and picturesque mountains, interspersed with a few tracts of fertile country, shut in between the sea and the ravine of the Jordan, and falling away into the waterless desert of the south. It was, too, a land of small extent, hardly more than one hundred and sixty miles in length and sixty miles in width. And even this amount of territory was possessed by the Israelites only during the reigns of David and Solomon. The sea-coast with its harbours was in the hands of the Phœnicians and the Philistines, and though the Philistines at one time owned an unwilling allegiance to the Jewish king, the Phœnicians preserved their independence, and even Solomon had to find harbours for his merchantmen, not on the coast of his own native kingdom, but in the distant Edomite ports of Eloth and Ezion-geber, in the Gulf of Aqabah. With the loss of Edom Judah ceased to have a foreign trade.

The Negeb, or desert of the south, was then, what it still is, the haunt of robbers and marauders. The Beduin of to-day are the Amalekites of Old Testament history ; and then, as now, they infested the southern frontier of Judah, wasting and robbing

the fields of the husbandman, and allying themselves with every invader who came from the south.
Saul, indeed, punished them, as Romans and
Turks have punished them since ; but the lesson
is remembered only for a short while : when the
strong hand is removed, the " sons of the desert "
return again like the locusts to their prey.

It is true that the Beduin now range over the
loamy plains and encamp among the marshes of
Lake Hûleh, where in happier times their presence
was unknown. But this is the result of a weak
and corrupt government, added to the depopula-
tion of the lowlands. There are traces even in
the Old Testament that in periods of anarchy and
confusion the Amalekites penetrated far into the
country in a similar fashion. In the Song of
Deborah and Barak Ephraim is said to have contended against them, and accordingly " Pirathon in
the land of Ephraim " is described as being " in the
mount of the Amalekites " (Judges xii. 15). In
the cuneiform tablets of Tel el-Amarna, too, there
is frequent mention of the " Plunderers " by whom
the Beduin, the Shasu of the Egyptian texts, must
be meant, and who seem to have been generally
ready at hand to assist a rebellious vassal or take
part in a civil feud.

Lebanon, the " white " mountain, took its name
from its cliffs of glistening limestone. In the early
days of Canaan it was believed to be the habitation of the gods, and Phœnician inscriptions exist
dedicated to Baal-Lebanon, " the Baal of Lebanon.'

He was the special form of the Sun-god whose seat was in the mountain-ranges that shut in Phœnicia on the east, and whose spirit was supposed to dwell in some mysterious way in the mountains themselves. But there were certain peaks which lifted themselves up prominently to heaven, and in which consequently the sanctity of the whole range was as it were concentrated. It was upon their summits that the worshipper felt himself peculiarly near the God of heaven, and where therefore the altar was built and the sacrifice performed. One of these peaks was Hermon, "the consecrated," whose name the Greeks changed into Harmonia, the wife of Agenor the Phœnician. From its top we can see Palestine spread as it were before us, and stretching southwards to the mountains of Judah. The walls of the temple, which in Greek times took the place of the primitive altar, can still be traced there, and on its slopes, or perched above its ravines, are the ruins of other temples of Baal—at Dêr el-'Ashair, at Rakleh, at Ain Hersha, at Rashêyat el-Fukhâr—all pointing towards the central sanctuary on the summit of the mountain.

The name of Hermon, "the consecrated," was but an epithet, and the mountain had other and more special names of its own. The Sidonians, we are told (Deut. iii. 9), called it Sirion, and another of its titles was Sion (Deut. iv. 48), unless indeed this is a corrupt reading for Sirion. Its Amorite name was Shenir (Deut. iii. 9), which appears as Saniru in an Assyrian inscription, and goes back to the earliest dawn of history. When the Babylonians first began to make expeditions against the West, long before the birth of Abraham, the name of Sanir was already known. It was then used to denote the whole of Syria, so that its restriction to Mount Hermon alone must have been of later date.

Another holy peak was Carmel, "the fruitful field," or perhaps originally "the domain of the god." It was in Mount Carmel that the mountain ranges of the north ended finally, and the altar on its summit could be seen from afar by the Phœnician sailors. Here the priests of Baal called in vain upon their god that he might send them rain, and here was "the altar of the Lord" which Elijah repaired.

The mountains of the south present no striking peak or headland like Hermon and Carmel. Even Tabor belongs to the north. Ebal and Gerizim alone, above Shechem, stand out among their fellows, and were venerated as the abodes of deity from the earliest times. The temple-hill at Jerusalem owed its sanctity rather to the city within the boundaries of which it stood than to its own character. In fact, the neighbouring height of Zion towered above it. The mountains of the south were rather highlands than lofty chains and isolated peaks.

But on this very account they played an important part in the history of the world. They were not too high to be habitable; they were high enough to protect their inhabitants against invasion and war. "Mount Ephraim," the block of mountainous land of which Shechem and Samaria formed the centre, and at the southern extremity of which the sacred city of Shiloh stood, was the natural nucleus of a kingdom, like the southern block of which Hebron and Jerusalem were similarly the capitals. Here there were valleys and uplands in which sufficient food could be grown for the needs of the population, while the cities with their thick and lofty walls were strongholds difficult to approach and still more difficult to capture. The climate was bracing, though the winters were cold, and it reared a race of hardy warriors and industrious agriculturists. The want of water was the only difficulty; in most cases the people were dependent on rain-water, which they preserved in cisterns cut out of the rock.

This block of southern mountains was the first and latest stronghold of Israel. It constituted, in fact, the kingdoms of Samaria and Judah. Out of it, at Shechem, came the first attempt to found a monarchy in Israel, and thus unite the Israelitish tribes; out of it also came the second and more successful attempt under Saul the Benjamite and David the Jew. The Israelites never succeeded in establishing themselves on the sea-coast, and their possession of the plain of Megiddo and the southern slopes of the Lebanon was a source of weakness and not of strength. It led eventually to the overthrow of the kingdom of Samaria. The northern

tribes in Galilee were absorbed by the older population, and their country became "Galilee of the
Gentiles," rather than an integral part of Israel.
The plain of Megiddo was long held by the
Canaanites, and up to the last was exposed to
invasion from the sea-coast. It was, in fact, the
battle-field of Palestine. The army of the invader
or the conqueror marched along the edge of the
sea, not through the rugged paths and dangerous
defiles of the mountainous interior, and the plain of
Megiddo was the pass which led them into its
midst. The possession of the plain cut off the
mountaineers of the north from their brethren in
the south, and opened the way into the heart of
the mountains themselves.

But to possess the plain was also to possess
chariots and horsemen, and a large and disciplined
force. The guerilla warfare of the mountaineer
was here of no avail. Success lay on the side of
the more numerous legions and the wealthier state,
on the side of the assailant and not of the
assailed.

Herein lay the advantage of the kingdom of
Judah. It was a compact state, with no level plain
to defend, no outlying territories to protect. Its
capital stood high upon the mountains, strongly
fortified by nature and difficult of access. While
Samaria fell hopelessly and easily before the armies
of Assyria, Jerusalem witnessed the fall of Nineveh
itself.

What was true of the later days of Israelitish

history was equally true of the age of the patriarchs. The strength of Palestine lay in its southern
highlands ; whoever gained possession of these was
master of the whole country, and the road lay open
before him to Sinai and Egypt. But to gain
possession of them was the difficulty, and campaign
after campaign was needed before they could be
reduced to quiet submission. In the time of the
eighteenth Egyptian dynasty Jerusalem was already
the key to Southern Palestine.

Geographically, Palestine was thus a country of
twofold character, and its population was necessarily twofold as well. It was a land of mountain
and plain, of broken highlands and rocky sea-coast.
Its people were partly mountaineers, active, patriotic,
and poor, with a tendency to asceticism ; partly
a nation of sailors and merchants, industrious,
wealthy, and luxurious, with no sense of country or
unity, and accounting riches the supreme end of
life. On the one hand, it gave the world its first
lessons in maritime exploration and trade ; on the
other it has been the religious teacher of mankind.

In both respects its geographical position has
aided the work of its people. Situated midway
between the two great empires of the ancient
Oriental world, it was at once the high road and
the meeting-place of the civilizations of Egypt and
Babylonia. Long before Abraham migrated to
Canaan it had been deeply interpenetrated by
Babylonian culture and religious ideas, and long

before the Exodus it had become an Egyptian province. It barred the way to Egypt for the invader from Asia ; it protected Asia from Egyptian assault. The trade of the world passed through it and met in it ; the merchants of Egypt and Ethiopia could traffic in Palestine with the traders of Babylonia and the far East. It was destined by nature to be a land of commerce and trade.

And yet while thus forming a highway from the civilization of the Euphrates to that of the Nile, Palestine was too narrow a strip of country to become itself a formidable kingdom. The empire of David scarcely lasted for more than a single generation, and was due to the weakness at the same time of both Egypt and Assyria. With the Arabian desert on the one side and the Mediterranean on the other, it was impossible for Canaan to develop into a great state. Its rocks and mountains might produce a race of hardy warriors and energetic thinkers, but they could not create a rich and populous community. The Phœnicians on the coast were driven towards the sea, and had to seek in maritime enterprise the food and wealth which their own land refused to grant. Palestine was essentially formed to be the appropriator and carrier of the ideas and culture of others, not to be itself their origin and creator.

But when the ideas had once been brought to it they were modified and combined, improved and generalized in a way that made them capable of universal acceptance. Phœnician art is in no way

C

original ; its elements have been drawn partly from Babylonia, partly from Egypt ; but their combination was the work of the Phœnicians, and it was just this combination which became the heritage of civilized man. The religion of Israel came from the wilderness, from the heights of Sinai, and the palm-grove of Kadesh, but it was in Palestine that it took shape and developed, until in the fullness of time the Messiah was born. Out of Canaan have come the Prophets and the Gospel, but the Law which lay behind them was brought from elsewhere.

CHAPTER II

THE PEOPLE

IN the days of Abraham, Chedor-laomer, king of Elam and lord over the kings of Babylonia, marched westward with his Babylonian allies, in order to punish his rebellious subjects in Canaan. The invading army entered Palestine from the eastern side of the Jordan. Instead of marching along the sea-coast, it took the line of the valley of the Jordan. It first attacked the plateau of Bashan, and then smote "the Rephaim in Ashteroth Karnaim, and the Zuzim in Ham, and the Emim in the plain of Kiriathaim." Then it passed into Mount Seir, and subjugated the Horites as far as El-Paran "by the wilderness." Thence it turned northward again through the oasis of En-mishpat or Kadesh-barnea, and after smiting the Amalekite Beduin, as well as the Amorites in Hazezon-tamar, made its way into the vale of Siddim. There the battle took place which ended in the defeat of the king of Sodom and his allies, who were carried away captive to the north. But at Hobah, "on the left hand of Damascus," the invaders were overtaken by "Abram the Hebrew," who dwelt with his Amorite confederates in the plain of Mamre, and the spoil they had seized was recovered from them.

The narrative gives us a picture of the geography and ethnology of Palestine as it was at the beginning of the Patriarchal Age. Before that age was over it had altered very materially; the old cities for the most part still remained, but new races had taken the place of the older ones, new kingdoms had arisen, and the earlier landmarks had been displaced. The Amalekite alone continued what he had always been, the untamable nomad of the southern desert.

Rephaim or "Giants" was a general epithet applied to the prehistoric population of the country. Og, king of Bashan in the time of the Exodus, was "of the remnant of the Rephaim" (Deut. iii. 11); but so also were the Anakim in Hebron, the Emim in Moab, and the Zamzummim in Ammon (Deut. ii. 11, 20). Doubtless they represented a tall race in comparison with the Hebrews and Arabs of the desert; and the Israelitish spies described themselves as grasshoppers by the side of them (Numb. xiii. 33). It is possible, however, that the name was really an ethnic one, which had only an accidental similarity in sound to the Hebrew word for "giants." At all events, in the list of conquered Canaanitish towns which the Pharaoh Thothmes III. of Egypt caused to be engraved on the walls of Karnak, the name of Astartu or Ashteroth

Karnaim is followed by that of Anaurepâ, in which Mr. Tomkins proposes to see On-Repha, "On of the Giant(s)." In the close neighbourhood in classical days stood Raphôn or Raphana, Arpha of the Dekapolis, now called Er-Râfeh, and in Raphôn it is difficult not to discern a reminiscence of the Rephaim of Genesis.

Did these Rephaim belong to the same race as the Emim and the Anakim, or were the latter called Rephaim or " Giants " merely because they represented the tall prehistoric population of Canaan ? The question can be more easily asked than answered. We know from the Book of Genesis that Amorites as well as Hittites lived at Hebron, or in its immediate vicinity. Abram dwelt in the plain of Mamre along with three Amorite chieftains, and Hoham, king of Hebron, who fought against Joshua, is accounted among the Amorites (Josh. x. 1). The Anakim may therefore have been an Amorite tribe. They held themselves to be the descendants of Anak, an ancient Canaanite god, whose female counterpart was the Phœnician goddess Onka. But, on the other hand, the Amorites at Hebron may have been intruders ; we know that Hebron was peculiarly a Hittite city, and it is at Mamre rather than at Hebron that the Amorite confederates of Abram had their home. It is equally possible that the Anakim themselves may have been the stranger element ; we hear nothing about them in the days of the patriarchs, and it is only when the Israelites prepare to enter

Canaan that they first make their appearance upon the stage.

Og, king of Bashan, however, was an Amorite ; of this we are assured in the Book of Deuteronomy (iii. 8), and it is further said of him that he only " remained of the remnant of the Rephaim." The expression is a noticeable one, as it implies that the older population had been for the most part driven out. And such, in fact, was the case. At Rabbath, the capital of Ammon, the basalt sarcophagus of the last king of Bashan was preserved ; but the king and his people had alike perished. Ammonites and Israelites had taken their place.

The children of Ammon had taken possession of the land once owned by the Zamzummim (Deut. ii. 20). The latter are called Zuzim in the narrative of Genesis, and they are said to have dwelt in Ham. But Zuzim and Ham are merely faulty transcriptions from a cuneiform text of the Hebrew Zamzummim and Ammon, and the same people are meant both in Genesis and in Deuteronomy. In Deuteronomy also the Emim are mentioned, and their geographical position defined. They were the predecessors of the Moabites, and like the Zamzummim, "a people great and many and tall," whom the Moabites expelled doubtless at the same time as that at which the Ammonites conquered the Zamzummim. The "plain of Kiriathaim," or "the two cities," must have lain south of the Arnon, where Ar and Kir Haraseth were built.

South of the Emim, in the rose-red mountains of Seir, afterwards occupied by the Edomites, came the Horites, whose name is generally supposed to be derived from a Hebrew word signifying "a cave." They have therefore been regarded as Troglodytes, or cave-dwellers, a savage race of men who possessed neither houses nor settled home. But it is quite possible to connect the name with another word which means "white," and to see in them the representatives of a white race. The name of Hor is associated with Beth-lehem, and Caleb, of the Edomite tribe of Kenaz, is called "the son of Hur" (1 Chron. ii. 50, iv. 4). There is no reason for believing that cave-dwellers ever existed in that part of Palestine.

The discovery of the site of Kadesh-barnea is due in the first instance to Dr. Rowlands, secondly to the archæological skill of Dr. Clay Trumbull. It is still known as 'Ain Qadîs, "the spring of Qadîs," and lies hidden within the block of mountains which rise in the southern desert about midway between Mount Seir and the Mediterranean Sea. The water still gushes out of the rock, fresh and clear, and nourishes the oasis that surrounds it. It has been marked out by nature to be a meeting-place and "sanctuary" of the desert tribes. Its central position, its security from sudden attack, and its abundant supply of water all combined to make it the En-Mishpat or "Spring of Judgment," where cases were tried and laws enacted. It was here that the Israelites lingered year after year

during their wanderings in the wilderness, and it
was from hence that the spies were sent out to
explore the Promised Land. In those days the
mountains which encircled it were known as "the
mountains of the Amorites" (Deut. i. 19, 20). In
the age of the Babylonian invasion, however, the
Amorites had not advanced so far to the south.
They were as yet only at Hazezon-tamar, the
"palm-grove" on the western shore of the Dead
Sea, which a later generation called En-gedi (2
Chron. xx. 2). En-Mishpat was still in the hands
of the Amalekites, the lords of "all the country"
round about.

The Amalekites had not as yet intermingled
with the Ishmaelites, and their Beduin blood was
still pure. They were the Shasu or "Plunderers"
of the Egyptian inscriptions, sometimes also
termed the Sitti, the Sute of the cuneiform texts.
Like their modern descendants, they lived by the
plunder of their more peaceful neighbours. As
was prophesied of Ishmael, so could it have been
prophesied of the Amalekites, that their "hand
should be against every man, and every man's
hand against" them. They were the wild offspring
of the wilderness, and accounted the first-born of
mankind (Numb. xxiv. 20).

From En-Mishpat the Babylonian forces marched
northward along the western edge of the Dead Sea.
Leaving Jerusalem on their left, they descended
into the vale of Siddim, where they found themselves
in the valley of the Jordan, and consequently in

the land of the Canaanites. As we are told in the
Book of Numbers (xiii. 29), while "the Amalekites
dwell in the land of the south, and the Hittites and
the Jebusites and Amorites dwell in the mountains,
the Canaanites dwell by the sea and by the coast
of Jordan."

The word Canaan, as we have seen, meant "the
lowlands," and appears sometimes in a longer,
sometimes in a shorter form. The shorter form is
written Khna by the Greeks : in the Tel el-Amarna
tablets it is Kinakhkhi, while Canaan, the longer
form, is Kinakhna. It is this longer form which
alone appears in the hieroglyphic texts. Here we
read how Seti I. destroyed the Shasu or Amalekites
from the eastern frontier of Egypt to "the land of
Kana'an," and captured their fortress of the same
name which Major Conder has identified with
Khurbet Kan'an near Hebron. It was also the
longer form which was preserved among the Israelites as well as among the Phœnicians, the original
inhabitants of the sea-coast. Coins of Laodicea,
on the Orontes, bear the inscription, " Laodicea a
metropolis in Canaan," and St. Augustine states that
in his time the Carthaginian peasantry of Northern
Africa, if questioned as to their descent, still
answered that they were " Canaanites." (*Exp.
Epist. ad Rom.* 13.)

In course of time the geographical signification
of the name came to be widely extended beyond
its original limits. Just as Philistia, the district of
the Philistines, became the comprehensive Palestine,

so Canaan, the land of the Canaanites of the coast
and the valley, came to denote the whole of the
country between the Jordan and the sea. It is
already used in this sense in the cuneiform correspondence of Tel el-Amarna. Already in the
century before the Exodus Kinakhna or Canaan
represented pretty nearly all that we now mean by
" Palestine." It was in fact the country to the
south of " the land of the Amorites," and " the land
of the Amorites " lay immediately to the north of
the Waters of Merom.

In the geographical table in the tenth chapter
of Genesis Canaan is stated to be the son of Ham
and the brother of Mizraim or Egypt. The statement indicates the age to which the account must
go back. There was only one period of history in
which Canaan could be geographically described as
a brother of Egypt, and that was the period of the
eighteenth and nineteenth dynasties, when for a
while it was a province of the Pharaohs. At no
other time was it closely connected with the sons
of Ham. At an earlier epoch its relations had
been with Babylonia rather than with the valley
of the Nile, and with the fall of the nineteenth
dynasty the Asiatic empire of Egypt came finally
to an end.

The city of Sidon, we are further told, was the
first-born of Canaan. It claimed to be the oldest
of the Phœnician cities in the " lowlands " of the
coast. It had grown out of an assemblage of
" fishermen's " huts, and Said the god of the fisher-

men continued to preside over it to the last. The fishermen became in time sailors and merchant-princes, and the fish for which they sought was the murex with its precious purple dye. Tyre, the city of the "rock," which in later days disputed the supremacy over Phœnicia with Sidon, was of younger foundation. Herodotus was told that the great temple of Baal Melkarth, "the city's king," which he saw there, had been built twenty-three centuries before his visit. But Sidon was still older, older even than Gebal, the sacred city of the goddess Baaltis.

The wider extension of the name of Canaan brought with it other geographical relationships besides those of the sea-coast. Hittites and Amorites, Jebusites and Girgashites, Hivites and the peoples of the southern Lebanon, were all settled within the limits of the larger Canaan, and were therefore accounted his sons. Even Hamath claimed the right to be included in the brotherhood. It is said with truth that "afterwards were the families of the Canaanites spread abroad."

Hittites and Amorites were interlocked both in the north and in the south. Kadesh, on the Orontes, the southern stronghold of the Hittite kingdom of the north, was, as the Egyptian records tell us, in the land of the Amorites; while in the south Hittites and Amorites were mingled together at Hebron, and Ezekiel (xvi. 3) declares that Jerusalem had a double parentage: its birth was in the land of Canaan, but its father was an

Amorite and its mother a Hittite. Modern research,
however, has shown that Hittites and Amorites
were races widely separated in character and
origin. About the Hittites we hear a good deal
both in the hieroglyphic and in the cuneiform
inscriptions. The Khata of the Egyptian texts
were the most formidable power of Western Asia
with whom the Egyptians of the eighteenth and
nineteenth dynasties had to deal. They were
tribes of mountaineers from the ranges of the
Taurus who had descended on the plains of Syria
and established themselves there in the midst
of an Aramaic population. Carchemish on the
Euphrates became one of their Syrian capitals,
commanding the high-road of commerce and war
from east to west. Thothmes III., the conqueror
of Western Asia, boasts of the gifts he received
from "the land of Khata the greater," so called, it
would seem, to distinguish it from another and
lesser land of Khata—that of the Hittites of the
south.

The cuneiform tablets of Tel el-Amarna, in the
closing days of the eighteenth dynasty, represent
the Hittites as advancing steadily southward and
menacing the Syrian possessions of the Pharaoh.
Disaffected Amorites and Canaanites looked to
them for help, and eventually "the land of the
Amorites" to the north of Palestine fell into their
possession. When the first Pharaohs of the nineteenth dynasty attempted to recover the Egyptian
empire in Asia, they found themselves confronted

by the most formidable of antagonists. Against Kadesh and "the great king of the Hittites" the Egyptian forces were driven in vain, and after twenty years of warfare Ramses II., the Pharaoh of the Oppression, was fain to consent to peace. A treaty of alliance, offensive and defensive, was drawn up between the two rivals, and Egypt was henceforth compelled to treat with the Hittites on equal terms.

The Khattâ or Khatâ of the Assyrian inscriptions are already a decaying power. They are broken into a number of separate states or kingdoms, of which Carchemish is the richest and most important. They are in fact in retreat towards those mountains of Asia Minor from which they had originally issued forth. But they still hold their ground in Syria for a long while. There were Hittites at Kadesh in the reign of David. Hittite kings could lend their services to Israel in the age of Elisha (2 Kings vii. 6), and it was not till B.C. 717 that Carchemish was captured by Sargon of Assyria, and the trade which passed through it diverted to Nineveh. But when the Assyrians first became acquainted with the coastland of the Mediterranean, the Hittites were to such an extent the ruling race there that they gave their name to the whole district. Like "Palestine," or "Canaan," the term "land of the Hittites" came to denote among the Assyrians, not only Northern Syria and the Lebanon, but Southern Syria as well. Even Ahab of Israel and Baasha the Ammonite are included by Shalmaneser II. among its kings.

This extended use of the name among the Assyrians is illustrated by the existence of a Hittite tribe at Hebron in the extreme south of Palestine. Various attempts have been made to get rid of the latter by unbelieving critics, but, the statements of Genesis are corroborated by Ezekiel's account of the foundation of Jerusalem. They are, moreover, in full harmony with the monumental records. As we have seen, Thothmes III. implies that already in his day there was a second and smaller land of the Hittites, and the great Babylonian work on astronomy contains references to the Hittites which appear to go back to early days.

Assyrian and Babylonian texts are not the only cuneiform records which make mention of the " Khata " or Hittites. Their name is found also on the monuments of the kings of Ararat or Armenia who reigned in the ninth and eighth centuries before our era, and who had borrowed from Nineveh the cuneiform system of writing. But the Khata of these Vannic or Armenian texts lived considerably to the north of the Hittites of the Bible and of the Egyptian and Assyrian monuments. The country they inhabited lay in eastern Asia Minor in the neighbourhood of the modern Malatiyeh. Here, in fact, was their original home.

Thanks to the Egyptian artists, we are well acquainted with the Hittite physical type. It was not handsome. The nose was unduly protrusive, while the chin and the forehead retreated. The cheeks were square with prominent bones, and the face was beardless. In colour the Hittites were yellow-skinned with black hair and eyes. They seem to have worn their hair in three long plaits which fell over the back like the pigtail of a Chinaman, and they were distinguished by the use of boots with upturned toes.

We might perhaps imagine that the Egyptian artists have caricatured their adversaries. But this is not the case. Precisely the same profile of face, sometimes even exaggerated in its ugliness, is represented on the Hittite monuments by the native sculptors themselves. It is one of the surest proofs we possess that these monuments, with their still undeciphered inscriptions, are of Hittite origin. They belong to the people whom Israelites, Egyptians, Assyrians, and Armenians united in calling Hittites.

In marked contrast to the Hittites stood the Amorites. They too are depicted on the walls of the Egyptian temples and tombs. While the Hittite type of features is Mongoloid, that of the Amorite is European. His nose is straight and somewhat pointed, his lips and nostrils thin, his cheek-bones high, his mouth firm and regular, his forehead expressive of intelligence. He has a fair amount of whisker, ending in a pointed beard. At Abu-Simbel the skin is painted a pale yellow— the Egyptian equivalent for white—his eyes blue, and his beard and eyebrows red. At Medînet

Habu, his skin, as Prof. Petrie expresses it, is "rather pinker than flesh-colour," while in a tomb of the eighteenth dynasty at Thebes it is painted white, the eyes and hair being a light red-brown.

The Amorite, it is clear, must be classed with the fair-skinned, blue-eyed Libyans of the Egyptian monuments, whose modern descendants are the Kabyles and other Berber tribes of Northern Africa. The latter are not only European in type, they claim special affinities to the blond, "golden-haired" Kelt. And their tall stature agrees well with what the Old Testament has to tell us about the Amorites. They too were classed among the Rephaim or "giants," by the side of whom the Israelite invaders were but as "grasshoppers."

While the Canaanites inhabited the lowlands, the highlands were the seat of the Amorites (Num. xiii. 29). This, again, is in accordance with their European affinities. They flourished best in the colder and more bracing climate of the mountains, as do the Berber tribes of Northern Africa to-day. The blond, blue-eyed race is better adapted to endure the cold than the heat.

Amorite tribes and kingdoms were to be found in all parts of Palestine. Southward, as we have seen, Kadesh-barnea was in "the mountain of the Amorites," while Chedor-laomer found them on the western shores of the Dead Sea. When Abraham pitched his tent in the plain above Hebron, it was in the possession of three Amorite chieftains, and at the time of the Israelitish conquest, Hebron and Jerusalem, Jarmuth, Lachish and Eglon were all Amorite (Josh. x. 5). Jacob assured Joseph the inheritance of his tribe should be in that district of Shechem which the patriarch had taken "out of the hand of the Amorite" (Gen. xlviii. 22), and on the eastern side of the Jordan were the Amorite kingdoms of Og and Sihon. But we learn from the Egyptian inscriptions, and more especially from the Tel el-Amarna tablets, that the chief seat of Amorite power lay immediately to the north of Palestine. Here was "the land of the Amorites," to which frequent reference is made by the monuments, among the ranges of Lebanon and Anti-Lebanon, from Hamath southward to Hermon. On the east it was bounded by the desert, on the west by the cities of Phœnicia.

In early days, long before the age of Abraham, the Amorites must already have been the predominant population in this part of Syria. When the Babylonian king, Sargon of Akkad, carried his victorious arms to the shores of the Mediterranean, it was against "the land of the Amorites" that his campaigns were directed. From that time forward this was the name under which Syria, and more particularly Canaan, was known to the Babylonians. The geographical extension of the term was parallel to that of " Hittites " among the Assyrians, of " Canaan " among the Israelites, and of " Palestine " among ourselves. But it bears witness to the important part which was played by the Amorites in what we must still call the prehistoric age of

D

Syria, as well as to the extent of the area which they must have occupied.

Of course it does not follow that the whole of this area was occupied at one and the same time. Indeed we know that the conquest of the northern portion of Moab by the Amorite king Sihon took place only a short time before the Israelitish invasion, and part of the Amorite song of triumph on the occasion has been preserved in the Book of Numbers. " There is a fire gone out of Heshbon," it said, " a flame from the city of Sihon : it hath consumed Ar of Moab, and the lords of the high places of Arnon. Woe to thee, Moab ! thou art undone, O people of Chemosh : he hath given his sons that escaped, and his daughters, into captivity unto Sihon king of the Amorites."[1]   In the south, again, the Amorites do not seem to have made their way beyond Hazezon-Tamar, while the Tel el-Amarna tablets make it probable that neither Bashan nor Jerusalem were as yet Amorite at the time they were written. It may be that the Amorite conquests in the south were one of the results of the fall of the Egyptian empire and the Hittite irruption.

Between the Hittite and the Amorite the geographical table of Genesis interposes the Jebusite, and the Book of Numbers similarly states that " the Hittites and the Jebusites and the Amorites dwell in the mountains." The Jebusites, however, were merely the local tribe which in the early days

---

[1] Num. xxi. 28, 29.

of the Israelitish occupation of Canaan were in possession of Jerusalem, and they were probably either Hittite or Amorite in race. At any rate there is no trace of them in the cuneiform letters of Tel el-Amarna. On the contrary, in these Jerusalem is still known only by its old name of Uru-salim ; of the name Jebus there is not a hint. But the letters show us that Ebed-Tob, the native king of Jerusalem and humble vassal of the Pharaoh, was being hard pressed by his enemies, and that, in spite of his urgent appeals for help, the Egyptians were unable to send any. His enemy were the Khabiri or " Confederates," about whose identification there has been much discussion, but who were assisted by the Beduin chief Labai and his sons. One by one the towns belonging to the territory of Jerusalem fell into the hands of his adversaries, and at last, as we learn from another letter, Ebed-Tob himself along with his capital was captured by the foe. It was this event, perhaps, which made Jerusalem a Jebusite city. If so, we must see in the enemies of Ebed-Tob the Jebusites of the Old Testament.

The Girgashite is named after the Amorite, but who he may have been it is hard to say. In the Egyptian epic composed by the court-poet Pentaur, to commemorate the heroic deeds of Ramses II. in his struggle with the Hittites, mention is twice made of " the country of Qarqish." It was one of those which had sent contingents to the Hittite army. But it seems to have been situated in

Northern Syria, if not in Asia Minor, so that unless we can suppose that some of its inhabitants had followed in the wake of the Hittites and settled in Palestine, it is not easy to see how they could be included among the sons of Canaan. The Hivites, whose name follows that of the Girgashites, are simply the "villagers" or fellahin as opposed to the townsfolk. They are thus synonymous with the Perizzites, who take their place in Gen. xv. 20, and whose name has the same signification. But whereas the Perizzites were especially the country population of Southern Palestine, the Hivites were those of the north. In two passages, indeed, the name appears to be used in an ethnic sense, once in Gen. xxxvi. 2, where we read that Esau married the granddaughter of "Zibeon the Hivite," and once in Josh. xi. 3, where reference is made to " the Hivite under Hermon in the land of Mizpeh." But a comparison of the first passage with a later part of the chapter (vv. 20, 24, 25) proves that "Hivite" is a corrupt reading for "Horite," while it is probable that in the second passage "Hittite" ought to be read for "Hivite."

The four last sons of Canaan represent cities, and not tribes. Arka, called Irqat in the Tel el-Amarna tablets, and now known as Tel 'Arqa, was one of the inland cities of Phœnicia, in the mountains between the Orontes and the sea. Sin, which is mentioned by Tiglath-pileser III., was in the same neighbourhood, as well as Zemar (now Sumra), which, like Arvad (the modern Ruâd), is named repeatedly in the Tel el-Amarna correspondence. It was at the time an important Phœnician fortress,— "perched like a bird upon the rock,"—and was under the control of the governor of Gebal. Arvad was equally important as a sea-port, and its ships were used for war as well as for commerce. As for Hamath (now Hamah), the Khamat and Amat of the Assyrian texts, it was already a leading city in the days of the eighteenth Egyptian dynasty. Thothmes III. includes it among his Syrian conquests under the name of Amatu, as also does Ramses III. The Hittite inscriptions discovered there go to show that, like Kadesh on the Orontes, it fell at one time into Hittite hands.

Such then was the ethnographical map of Palestine in the Patriarchal Age. Canaanites in the lowlands, Amorites and Hittites in the highlands contended for the mastery. In the desert of the south were the Amalekite Beduin, ever ready to raid and murder their settled neighbours. The mountains of Seir were occupied by the Horites, while prehistoric tribes, who probably belonged to the Amorite race, inhabited the plateau east of the Jordan.

This was the Palestine to which Abraham migrated, but it was a Palestine which his migration was destined eventually to change. Before many generations had passed Moab and Ammon, the children of his nephew, took the place of the older population of the eastern table-land, while Edom settled in Mount Seir. A few generations more, and Israel too entered into its inheritance in Canaan itself. The Amorites were extirpated or became tributary, and the valleys of the Jordan and Kishon were seized by the invading tribes. The cities of the extreme south had already become Philistine, and the strangers from Caphtor had supplanted in them the Avim of an earlier epoch.

Meanwhile the waves of foreign conquest had spread more than once across the country. Canaan had been made subject to Babylonia, and had received in exchange for its independence the gift of Babylonian culture. Next it was Egypt which entered upon its career of Asiatic conquest, and Canaan for a while was an Egyptian province. But the Egyptian dominion in its turn passed away, and Palestine was left the prey of other assailants, of the Hittites and the Beduin, of the people of Aram Naharaim and the northern hordes. Egyptians and Babylonians, Hittites and Mesopotamians mingled with the earlier races of the country and obliterated the older landmarks. Before the Patriarchal Age came to an end, the ethnographical map of Canaan had undergone a profound change.

CHAPTER III

IT is in the cuneiform records of Babylonia that we catch the first glimpse of the early history of Canaan. Babylonia was not yet united under a single head. From time to time some prince arose whose conquests allowed him to claim the imperial title of " king of Sumer and Akkad," of Southern and Northern Babylonia, but the claim was never of long duration, and often it signified no more than a supremacy over the other rulers of the country.

It was while Babylonia was thus divided into more than one kingdom, that the first Chaldæan empire of which we know was formed by the military skill of Sargon of Akkad. Sargon was of Semitic origin, but his birth seems to have been obscure. His father, Itti-Bel, is not given the title of king, and the later legends which gathered around his name declared that his mother was of low degree, that his father he knew not, and that his father's brother lived in the mountain-land. Born in secrecy in the city of Azu-pirani, " whence the elephants issue forth," he was launched by his mother on the waters of the Euphrates in an ark of bulrushes daubed with pitch. The river carried the child to Akki the irrigator, who had compassion upon it, and brought it up as his own son. So Sargon became an agriculturist and gardener like his adopted father, till the goddess Istar beheld and loved him, and eventually gave him his kingdom and crown.

Whatever may have been the real history of Sargon's rise to power, certain it is that he showed himself worthy of it. He built himself a capital, which perhaps was Akkad near Sippara, and there founded a library stocked with books on clay and well provided with scribes. The standard works on astronomy and terrestrial omens were compiled for it, the first of which was translated into Greek by Berossos in days long subsequent. But it was as a conqueror and the founder of the first Semitic empire in Western Asia that posterity chiefly remembered him. He overthrew his rivals at home, and made himself master of Northern Babylonia. Then he marched into Elam on the east, and devastated its fields. Next he turned his attention to the west. Four times did he make his way to "the land of the Amorites," until at last it was thoroughly subdued. His final campaign occupied three years. The countries "of the sea of the setting sun" acknowledged his dominion, and he united them with his former conquests into "a single" empire. On the shores of the Mediterranean he erected images of himself in token of his victories, and caused the spoil of Cyprus "to pass over into the countries of the sea." Towards the end of his reign a revolt broke out against him in Babylonia, and he was besieged in the city of Akkad, but he "issued forth and smote" his enemies and utterly destroyed them. Then came his last campaign against Northern Mesopotamia, from which he returned with abundant prisoners and spoil.

Sargon's son and successor was Naram-Sin, "the beloved of the Moon-god," who continued the conquests of his father. His second campaign was against the land of Magan, the name under which Midian and the Sinaitic peninsula were known to the Babylonians. The result of it was the addition of Magan to his empire and the captivity of its king.

The copper mines of Magan, which are noticed in an early Babylonian geographical list, made its acquisition coveted alike by Babylonians and Egyptians. We find the Pharaohs of the third dynasty already establishing their garrisons and colonies of miners in the province of Mafkat, as they called it, and slaughtering the Beduin who interfered with them. The history of Naram-Sin shows that its conquest was equally an object of the Babylonian monarchs at the very outset of their history. But whereas the road from Egypt to Sinai was short and easy, that from Babylonia was long and difficult. Before a Babylonian army

could march into the peninsula it was needful that
Syria should be secure in the rear.   The conquest
of Palestine, in fact, was necessary before the
copper mines of Sinai could fall into Babylonian
hands.

The consolidation of Sargon's empire in the
west, therefore, was needful before the invasion of
the country of Magan could take place, and the
invasion accordingly was reserved for Naram-Sin
to make.   The father had prepared the way ; the
son obtained the great prize—the source of the
copper that was used in the ancient world.

The fact that the whole of Syria is described in
the annals of Sargon as " the land of the Amorites,"
implies, not only that the Amorites were the ruling
population in the country, but also that they must
have extended far to the south.   The " land of the
Amorites " formed the basis and starting-point for
the expedition of Naram-Sin into Magan ; it must,
therefore, have reached to the southern border of
Palestine, if not even farther.   The road trodden
by his forces would have been the same as that
which was afterwards traversed by Chedor-laomer,
and would have led him through Kadesh-barnea.
Is it possible that the Amorites were already in
possession of the mountain-block within which
Kadesh stood, and that this was their extreme
limit to the south ?

There were other names by which Palestine and
Syria were known to the early Babylonians, besides
the general title of " the land of the Amorites."

One of these was Tidanum or Tidnum ; another was Sanir or Shenir. There was yet another, the reading of which is uncertain, though it may be Khidhi or Titi.

Mr. Boscawen has pointed out a coincidence that is at least worthy of attention. The first Babylonian monarch who penetrated into the peninsula of Sinai bore a name compounded with that of the Moon-god, which thus bears witness to a special veneration for that deity. Now the name of Mount Sinai is similarly derived from that of the Babylonian Moon-god Sin. It was the high place where the god must have been adored from early times under his Babylonian name. It thus points to Babylonian influence, if not to the presence of Babylonians on the spot. Can it have been that the mountain whereon the God of Israel afterwards revealed Himself to Moses was dedicated to the Moon-god of Babylon by Naram-Sin the Chaldæan conqueror?

If such indeed were the case, it would have been more than two thousand years before the Israelitish exodus. Nabonidos, the last king of the later Babylonian empire, who had a fancy for antiquarian exploration, tells us that Naram-Sin reigned 3200 years before his own time, and therefore about 3750 B.C. The date, startlingly early as it seems to be, is indirectly confirmed by other evidence, and Assyriologists consequently have come to accept it as approximately correct.

How long Syria remained a part of the empire

of Sargon of Akkad we do not know. But it must
have been long enough for the elements of Babylonian culture to be introduced into it. The small
stone cylinders used by the Babylonians for sealing
their clay documents thus became known to the
peoples of the West. More than one has been
found in Syria and Cyprus which go back to the
age of Sargon and Naram-Sin, while there are
numerous others which are more or less barbarous
attempts on the part of the natives to imitate the
Babylonian originals. But the imitations prove
that with the fall of Sargon's empire the use of
seal-cylinders in Syria, and consequently of documents for sealing, did not disappear. That knowledge of writing, which was a characteristic of
Babylonian civilization, must have been carried with
it to the shores of the Mediterranean.

The seal-cylinders were engraved, sometimes
with figures of men and gods, sometimes with
symbols only. Very frequently lines of cuneiform
writing were added, and a common formula gave
the name of the owner of the seal, along with
those of his father and of the deity whom he worshipped. One of the seal-cylinders found in
Cyprus describes the owner as an adorer of " the
god Naram-Sin." It is true that its workmanship
shows it to belong to a much later date than the
age of Naram-Sin himself, but the legend equally
shows that the name of the conqueror of Magan
was still remembered in the West. Another
cylinder discovered in the Lebanon mentions " the

gods of the Amorite," while a third from the same
locality bears the inscription : " Multal-ili, the son
of Ili-isme-anni, the worshipper of the god Nin-si-
zida." The name of the god signified in the old
pre-Semitic language of Chaldæa " the lord of the
upright horn," while it is worth notice that the
names of the owner and his father are compounded
simply with the word *ili* or *el*, " god," not with the
name of any special divinity. Multal-ili means
" Provident is God," Ili-isme-anni, " O my God, hear
me ! "

Many centuries have to elapse before the monuments of Babylonia again throw light on the
history of Canaan. Somewhere about B.C. 2700,
a high-priest was ruling in a city of Southern
Babylonia, under the suzerainty of Dungi, the king
of Ur. The high-priest's name was Gudea, and
his city (now called Tel-loh by the Arabs) was
known as Lagas. The excavations made here by
M. de Sarzec have brought to light temples and
palaces, collections of clay books and carved stone
statues, which go back to the early days of Babylonian history. The larger and better part of the
monuments belong to Gudea, who seems to have
spent most of his life in building and restoring the
sanctuaries of the gods. Diorite statues of the
prince are now in the Louvre, and inscriptions
upon them state that the stone out of which they
were made was brought from the land of Magan.
On the lap of one of them is a plan of the royal
palace, with the scale of measurement marked on

the edge of a sort of drawing-board. Prof. Petrie
has shown that the unit of measurement represented in it is the cubit of the pyramid-builders of
Egypt.

The diorite of Sinai was not the only material
which was imported into Babylonia for the buildings
of Gudea. Beams of cedar and box were brought
from Mount Amanus at the head of the Gulf of
Antioch, blocks of stone were floated down the
Euphrates from Barsip near Carchemish, gold-dust
came from Melukhkha, the "salt" desert to the
east of Egypt which the Old Testament calls
Havilah ; copper was conveyed from the north of
Arabia, limestone from the Lebanon ("the mountains of Tidanum"), and another kind of stone
from Subsalla in the mountains of the Amorite
land. Before beams of wood and blocks of stone
could thus be brought from the distant West, it was
necessary that trade between Babylonia and the
countries of the Mediterranean should have long
been organized, that the roads throughout Western
Asia should have been good and numerous, and
that Babylonian influence should have been
extended far and wide. The conquests of Sargon
and Naram-Sin had borne fruit in the commerce
that had followed upon them.

Once more the curtain falls, and Canaan is
hidden for a while out of our sight. Babylonia has
become a united kingdom with its capital and
centre at Babylon. Khammurabi (B.C. 2356—2301)
has succeeded in shaking off the suzerainty of

Elam, in overthrowing his rival Eri-Aku, king of Larsa, with his Elamite allies, and in constituting himself sole monarch of Babylonia. His family seems to have been in part, if not wholly, of South Arabian extraction. Their names are Arabian rather than Babylonian, and the Babylonian scribes found a difficulty in transcribing them correctly. But once in the possession of the Babylonian throne, they became thoroughly national, and under Khammurabi the literary glories of the court of Sargon of Akkad revived once more.

Ammi-satana, the great-grandson of Khammurabi, calls himself king of "the land of the Amorites." Babylonia, therefore, still claimed to be paramount in Palestine. Even the name of the king is an indication of his connection with the West. Neither of the elements of which it is composed belonged to the Babylonian language. The first of them, Ammi, was explained by the Babylonian philologists as meaning "a family," but it is more probable that it represents the name of a god. We find it in the proper names both of Southern and of Northwestern Arabia. The early Minæan inscriptions of Southern Arabia contain names like Ammi-karib, Ammi-zadiqa, and Ammi-zaduq, the last of which is identical with that of Ammi-zaduq, the son and successor of Ammi-satana. The Egyptian Sinuhit, who in the time of the twelfth dynasty fled, like Moses, for his life from the court of the Pharaoh to the Kadmonites east of the Jordan, found protection among them at the hands of their chieftain Ammu-

ânshi. The Ammonites themselves were the "sons
of Ammi," and in numerous Hebrew names we
find that of the god. Ammi-el, Ammi-nadab, and
Ammi-shaddai are mentioned in the Old Testament, the Assyrian inscriptions tell us of Ammi-
nadab the king of Ammon, and it is possible that
even the name of Balaam, the Aramæan seer, may
be compounded with that of the god. At all
events, the city of Pethor from which he came was
"by the river (Euphrates) of the land of the children of Ammo," for such is the literal rendering of
the Hebrew words.

Ammi-satana was not the first of his line whose
authority had been acknowledged in Palestine.
The inscription in which he records the fact is but
a confirmation of what had been long known to us
from the Book of Genesis. There we read how
Chedor-laomer, the king of Elam, with the three
vassal princes, Arioch of Ellasar, Amraphel of
Shinar, and Tidal of Goyyim invaded Canaan, and
how the kings of the vale of Siddim with its pits
of asphalt became their tributaries. For thirteen
years they remained submissive and then rebelled.
Thereupon the Babylonian army again marched to
the west. Bashan and the eastern bank of the
Jordan were subjugated, the Horites in Mount Seir
were smitten, and the invaders then turned back
through Kadesh-barnea, overthrowing the Amalekites and the Amorites on their way. Then came
the battle in the vale of Siddim, which ended in
the defeat of the Canaanites, the death of the kings

of Sodom and Gomorrha, and the capture of abundant booty. Among the prisoners was Lot, the
nephew of Abram, and it was to effect his rescue
that the patriarch armed his followers and started
in pursuit of the conquerors. Near Damascus he
overtook them, and falling upon them by night,
recovered the spoil of Sodom as well as his
" brother's son."

Arioch is the Eri-Aku of the cuneiform texts.
In the old language of Chaldea the name signified
" servant of the Moon-god." The king is well
known to us from contemporaneous inscriptions.
Besides the inscribed bricks which have come from
the temple of the Moon-god which he enlarged in
the city of Ur, there are numerous contract tablets
that are dated in his reign. He tells us that he
was the son of an Elamite, Kudur-Mabug, son of
Simti-silkhak, and prince (or " father ") of Yamutbal on the borders of Elam and Babylonia. But
this is not all. He further gives Kudur-Mabug
the title of " father of the Amorite land." What
this title exactly means it is difficult to say ; one
thing, however, is certain, Kudur-Mabug must have
exercised some kind of power and authority in the
distant West.

His name, too, is remarkable. Names compounded with Kudur, " a servant," were common
in the Elamite language, the second element of the
name being that of a deity, to whose worship the
owner of it was dedicated. Thus we have Kudur-
Lagamar, " the servant of the god Lagamar," Kudur-

E

Nakhkhunte, "the servant of Nakhkhunte." But Mabug was not an Elamite divinity. It was, on the contrary, a Mesopotamian deity from whom the town of Mabug near Carchemish, called Bambykê by the Greeks, and assimilated by the Arabs to their Membij, "a source," derived its name. Can it be from this Syrian deity that the father of Arioch received his name?

The capital of Arioch or Eri-Aku was Larsa, the city of the Sun-god, now called Senkereh. With the help of his Elamite kindred, he extended his power from thence over the greater part of Southern Babylonia. The old city of Ur, once the seat of the dominant dynasty of Chaldæan kings, formed part of his dominions; Nipur, now Niffer, fell into his hands like the seaport Eridu on the shores of the Persian Gulf, and in one of his inscriptions he celebrates his conquest of "the ancient city of Erech." On the day of its capture he erected in gratitude a temple to his god Ingirisa, "for the preservation of his life."

But the god did not protect him for ever. A time came when Khammurabi, king of Babylon, rose in revolt against the Elamite supremacy, and drove the Elamite forces out of the land. Eri-Aku was attacked and defeated, and his cities fell into the hands of the conqueror. Khammurabi became sole king of Babylonia, which from henceforth obeyed but a single sceptre.

Are we to see in the Amraphel of Genesis the Khammurabi of the cuneiform inscriptions? The difference in the names seems to make it impossible. Moreover, Amraphel, we are told, was king of Shinar, and it is not certain that the Shinar of the fourteenth chapter of Genesis was that part of Babylonia of which Babylon was the capital. This, in fact, was the northern division of the country, and if we are to identify the Shinar of scripture with the Sumer of the monuments, as Assyriologists have agreed to do, Shinar would have been its southern half. It is true that in the later days of Hebrew history Shinar denoted the whole plain of Chaldæa, including the city of Babylon, but this may have been an extension of the meaning of the name similar to that of which Canaan is an instance.

Unless Sumer and Shinar are the same words, outside the Old Testament there is only one Shinar known to ancient geography. That was in Mesopotamia. The Greek geographers called it Singara (now Sinjar), an oasis in the midst of deserts, and formed by an isolated mountain tract abounding in springs. It is already mentioned in the annals of the Egyptian conqueror Thothmes III. In his thirty-third year (B.C. 1470), the king of Sangar sent him tribute consisting of lapis-lazuli "of Babylon," and of various objects carved out of it. From Sangar also horses were exported into Egypt, and in one of the Tel el-Amarna letters, the king of Alasiya in Northern Syria writes to the Pharaoh,— " Do not set me with the king of the Hittites and the king of Sankhar ; whatever gifts they have

sent to me I will restore to thee twofold." In hieroglyphic and cuneiform spelling, Sangar and Sankhar
are the exact equivalents of the Hebrew Shinar.

How the name of Shinar came to be transferred
from Mesopotamia to Babylonia is a puzzle. The
Mesopotamian Shinar is nowhere near the Babylonian frontier. It lies in a straight line westward
of Mosul and the ancient Nineveh, and not far
from the banks of the Khabur. Can its application
to Babylonia be due to a confusion between Sumer
and Sangar?

Whatever the explanation may be, it is clear that
the position of the kingdom of Amraphel is by no
means so easily determined as has hitherto been
supposed. It may be Sumer or Southern Babylonia; it may be Northern Babylonia with its capital Babylon; or again, it may be the Mesopotamian
oasis of Sinjar. Until we find the name of
Amraphel in the cuneiform texts it is impossible
to attain certainty.

There is one fact, however, which seems to
indicate that it really is either Sumer or Northern
Babylonia that is meant. The narrative of Chedor-
laomer's campaign begins with the words that it
took place " in the time of Amraphel, king of
Shinar." Chedor-laomer the Elamite was the
leader of the expedition; he too was the suzerain
lord of his allies; and nevertheless the campaign is
dated, not in his reign, but in that of one of the
subject kings. That the narrative has been taken
from the Babylonian annals there is little room for

doubt, and consequently it would follow from the dating that Amraphel was a Babylonian prince, perhaps that he was the ruler of the city which, from the days of Khammurabi onward, became the capital of the country. In that case we should have to find some way of explaining the difference between the Hebrew and the Babylonian forms of the royal name.

Lagamar or Lagamer, written Laomer in Hebrew, was one of the principal deities of Elam, and the Babylonians made him a son of their own water-god Ea. The Elamite king Chedor-laomer, or Kudur-Lagamar, as his name was written in his own language, must have been related to the Elamite prince Kudur-Mabug, whose son Arioch was a subject-ally of the Elamite monarch. Possibly they were brothers, the younger brother receiving as his share of power the title of "father" —not "king"—of Yamutbal and the land of the Amorites. At any rate it is a son of Kudur-Mabug and not of the Elamite sovereign who receives a principality in Babylonia.

In the Book of Genesis Arioch is called "king of Ellasar." But Ellasar is clearly the Larsa of the cuneiform inscriptions, perhaps with the word *al*, "city," prefixed. Larsa, the modern Senkereh, was in Southern Babylonia, on the eastern bank of the Euphrates, not far from Erech, and to the north of Ur. Its king was virtually lord of Sumer, but he claimed to be lord also of the north. In his inscriptions Eri-Aku assumes the imperial title of "king of Sumer and Akkad," of both divisions of Babylonia, and it may be that at one time the rival king of Babylon acknowledged his supremacy. Who " Tidal king of Goyyim " may have been we cannot tell. Sir Henry Rawlinson has proposed to see in Goyyim a transformation of Gutiùm, the name by which Kurdistan was called in early Babylonia. Mr. Pinches has recently discovered a cuneiform tablet in which mention is made, not only of Eri-Aku and Kudur-Lagamar, but also of Tudkhul, and Tudkhul would be an exact transcription in Babylonian of the Hebrew Tidal. But the tablet is mutilated, and its relation to the narrative of Genesis is not yet clear. For the present, therefore, we must leave Tidal unexplained.

The name even of one of the Canaanite kings who were subdued by the Babylonian army has found its confirmation in a cuneiform inscription. This is the name of " Shinab, king of Admah." We hear from Tiglath-pileser III. of Sanibu, king of Ammon, and Sanibu and Shinab are one and the same. The old name of the king of Admah was thus perpetuated on the eastern side of the Jordan.

It may be that the asphalt of Siddim was coveted by the Babylonian kings. Bitumen, it is true, was found in Babylonia itself near Hit, but if Amiaud is right, one of the objects imported from abroad for Gudea of Lagas was asphalt. It came from Madga, which is described as being "in the mountains of the river Gur(?)ruda." But no reference to the place is to be met with anywhere else in cuneiform literature.

When Abram returned with the captives and spoil of Sodom, the new king came forth to meet him "at the valley of Shaveh, which is the king's dale." This was in the near neighbourhood of Jerusalem, as we gather from the history of Absalom (2 Sam. xviii. 18). Accordingly we further read that at the same time "Melchizedek, king of Salem," and "priest of the most High God," "brought forth bread and wine," and blessed the Hebrew conqueror, who thereupon gave him tithes of all the spoil.

It is only since the discovery and decipherment of the cuneiform tablets of Tel el-Amarna that the story of Melchizedek has been illustrated and explained. Hitherto it had seemed to stand alone. The critics, in the superiority of their knowledge, had refused credit to it, and had denied that the name even of Jerusalem or Salem was known before the age of David. But the monuments have come to our help, and have shown that it is the critics and not the Biblical writer who have been in error.

Several of the most interesting of the Tel el-Amarna letters were written to the Pharaoh Amenôphis IV. Khu-n-Aten by Ebed-Tob the king of Jerusalem. Not only is the name of Uru-salim or Jerusalem the only one in use, the city itself is already one of the most important fortresses of Canaan. It was the capital of a large district which extended southwards as far as Keilah and Karmel of Judah. It commanded the approach to the vale of Siddim, and in one of his letters Ebed-Tob speaks of having repaired the royal roads not only in the mountains, but also in the *kikar* or "plain" of Jordan (Gen. xiii. 10). The possession of Jerusalem was eagerly coveted by the enemies of Ebed-Tob, whom he calls also the enemies of the Egyptian king.

Now Ebed-Tob declares time after time that he is not an Egyptian governor, but a tributary ally and vassal of the Pharaoh, and that he had received his royal power, not by inheritance from his father or mother, but through the arm (or oracle) of "the Mighty King." As "the Mighty King" is distinguished from the "great King" of Egypt, we must see in him the god worshipped by Ebed-Tob, the "Most High God" of Melchizedek, and the prototype of "the Mighty God" of Isaiah. It is this same mighty king, Ebed-Tob assures the Pharaoh in another letter, who will overthrow the navies of Babylonia and Aram-Naharaim.

Here, then, as late as the fifteenth century before our era we have a king of Jerusalem who owes his royal dignity to his god. He is, in fact, a priest as well as a king. His throne has not descended to him by inheritance ; so far as his kingly office is concerned, he is like Melchizedek, without father and without mother. Between Ebed-Tob and Melchizedek there is more than analogy ; there is a striking and unexpected resemblance. The description given of him by Ebed-Tob explains what has puzzled us so long in the person of Melchizedek.

The origin of the name of Jerusalem also is now cleared up. It was no invention of the age of David ; on the contrary, it goes back to the period of Babylonian intercourse with Canaan. It is written in the cuneiform documents Uru-Salim, " the city of Salim," the god of peace. One of the lexical tablets from the library of Nineveh has long ago informed us that in one of the languages known to the Babylonians *uru* was the equivalent of the Babylonian *alu*, " a city," and we now know that this language was that of Canaan. It would even seem that the word had 'originally been brought from Babylonia itself in the days when Babylonian writing and culture first penetrated to the West. In the Sumerian or pre-Semitic language of Chaldæa *eri* signified a "city," and *eri* in the pronunciation of the Semites became *uru*. Hence it was that Uru or Ur, the birthplace of Abraham, received its name at a time when it was the ruling city of Babylonia, and though the Semitic Babylonians themselves never adopted the word in common life it made its way to Canaan. The rise of the " city " in the west was part of that Babylonian civilization which was carried to the shores of the Mediterranean, and so the word which denoted it was borrowed from the old language of Chaldæa, like the word for " palace," *hêkâl*, the Sumerian *ê-gal*, or " Great House." It is noteworthy that Harran, the resting-place of Abraham on his way from Ur to Palestine, the half-way house, as it were, between East and West, also derived its name from a Sumerian word which signified "the high-road." *Harran* and *Ur* were two of the gifts which passed to Canaan from the speakers of the primæval language of Chaldæa.

We can now understand why Melchizedek should have been called the "king of Salem." His capital could be described either as Jeru-salem or as the city of Salem. And that it was often referred to as Salem simply is shown by the Egyptian monuments. One of the cities of Southern Palestine, the capture of which is represented by Ramses II. on the walls of the Ramesseum at Thebes, is Shalam or Salem, and "the district of Salem" is mentioned between "the country of Hadashah" (Josh. xv. 37) and "the district of the Dead Sea" and "the Jordan," in the list of the places which Ramses III. at Medînet Habu describes himself as having conquered in the same part of the world.

It may be that Isaiah is playing upon the old name of Jerusalem when he gives the Messiah the title of "Prince of Peace." But in any case the fact that Salim, the god of peace, was the patron deity of Jerusalem, lends a special significance to Melchizedek's treatment of Abram. The patriarch had returned in peace from an expedition in which he had overthrown the invaders of Canaan; he had restored peace to the country of the priest-king, and had driven away its enemies. The offering of bread and wine on the part of Melchizedek was a sign of freedom from the enemy and of gratitude to the deliverer, while the tithes paid by Abram were equally a token that the land was again at peace. The name of Salim, the god of peace, was under one form or another widely spread in the Semitic world. Salamanu, or Solomon, was the king of Moab in the time of Tiglath-pileser III.; the name of Shalmaneser of Assyria is written Sulman-asarid, "the god Sulman is chief," in the cuneiform inscriptions; and one of the Tel el-Amarna letters was sent by Ebed-Sullim, "the servant of Sullim," who was governor of Hazor. In one of the Assyrian cities (Dimmen-Silim, "the foundation-stone of peace") worship was paid to the god "Sulman the fish." Nor must we forget that "Salma was the father of Beth-lehem" (1 Chron. ii. 51).

In the time of the Israelitish conquest the king of Jerusalem was Adoni-zedek (Josh. x. 1). The name is similar to that of Melchi-zedek, though the exact interpretation of it is a matter of doubt. It points, however, to a special use of the word *zedek*, "righteousness," and it is therefore interesting to find the word actually employed in one of the letters of Ebed-Tob. He there says of the Pharaoh: "Behold, the king is righteous (*zaduq*) towards me." What makes the occurrence of the word the more striking is that it was utterly unknown to the Babylonians. The root *zadaq*, "to be righteous," did not exist in the Assyrian language.

There is yet another point in the history of the meeting between Abram and Melchizedek which must not be passed over. When the patriarch returned after smiting the invading army he was met outside Jerusalem not only by Melchizedek, but also by the new king of Sodom. It was, therefore, in the mountains and in the shadow of the sanctuary of the Most High God that the newly-appointed prince was to be found, rather than in the vale of Siddim. Does not this show that the king of Jerusalem already exercised that sovereignty over the surrounding district that Ebed-Tob did in the century before the Exodus? As we have seen, Ebed-Tob describes himself as re-pairing the roads in that very "Kikar," or "plain," in which Sodom and Gomorrha stood. It would seem then that the priest-king of the great fortress in the mountains was already acknowledged as the dominant Canaanitish ruler, and that the neighbour-ing princes had to pay him homage when they first received the crown. This would be an additional reason for the tithes given to him by Abram.

Long after the defeat of Chedor-laomer and his allies, if we are to accept the traditional belief, Abraham was again destined to visit Jerusalem. But he had ceased to be "Abram the Hebrew," the confederate of the Amorite chieftains in the plain of Mamre, and had become Abraham the father of the promised seed. Isaac had been born to him, and he was called upon to sacrifice his first-born son.

The place of sacrifice was upon one of the mountains in the land of Moriah. There at the last moment the hand of the father was stayed, and a ram was substituted for the human victim. "And Abraham called the name of that place Yahveh-yireh ; as it is said to this day, In the mount of the Lord it shall be seen." According to the Hebrew text of the Chronicles (2 Chron. iii. 1), this mount of the Lord where Abraham's sacrifice was offered was the temple-mount at Jerusalem. The proverb quoted in Genesis seems to indicate the same fact. Moreover, the distance of the mountain from Beer-sheba—three days' journey— would be also the distance of Jerusalem from Abraham's starting-place.

It is even possible that in the name of Yahveh-yireh we have a play upon the first element in the name of Jeru-salem. The word *uru*, "city," became *yeru* or *yiru* in Hebrew pronunciation, and between this and *yireh* the difference is not great. Yahveh-yireh, "the Lord sees," might also be interpreted "the Lord of Yeru."

The temple-hill was emphatically "the mount of the Lord." In Ezekiel (xliii. 15) the altar that stood upon it is called Har-el, "the mountain of God." The term reminds us of Babylonia, where the mercy-seat of the great temple of Bel-Merodach at Babylon was termed Du-azagga, "the holy hill." It was on this "seat of the oracles," as it was termed, that the god enthroned himself at the beginning of each year, and announced his will to mankind. But the mercy-seat was entitled "the holy hill" only because it was a miniature copy of "the holy hill" upon which the whole temple was erected. So, too, at Jerusalem, the altar is called "the mount of God" by Ezekiel only because it represents that greater "mount of God" upon which it was built. The temple-hill itself was the primitive Har-el.

The list of conquered localities in Palestine recorded by Thothmes III. at Karnak gives indirect testimony to the same fact. The name of Rabbah of Judah is immediately preceded in it by that of Har-el, "the mount of God." The position of this Har-el leads us to the very mountain tract in the midst of which Jerusalem stood. We now know that Jerusalem was already an important city in the age of the eighteenth Egyptian dynasty, and that it formed one of the Egyptian conquests; it would be strange therefore if no notice had been taken of it by the compiler of the list. May we not see, then, in the Har-el of the Egyptian scribe the sacred mountain of Israelitish history?

There is a passage in one of the letters of Ebed-Tob which may throw further light on the history of the temple-hill. Unfortunately one of the cuneiform characters in it is badly formed, so that its reading is not certain, and still more unfortunately this character is one of the most important in the whole paragraph. If Dr. Winckler and myself are right in our copies, Ebed-Tob speaks of "the city of the mountain of Jerusalem, the city of the temple

of the god Nin-ip, (whose) name (there) is Salim,
the city of the king." What we read "Salim,"
however, is read differently by Dr. Zimmern, so
that according to his copy the passage must be
translated : "the city of the mountain of Jerusalem,
the city of the temple of the god Nin-ip is its
name, the city of the king." In the one case Ebed-
Tob will state explicitly that the god of Jerusalem,
whom he identifies with the Babylonian Nin-ip, is
Salim or Sulman, the god of peace, and that his
temple stood on "the mountain of Jerusalem";
in the other case there will be no mention of
Salim, and it will be left doubtful whether or
not the city of Beth-Nin-ip was included within the walls of the capital. It would seem
rather that it was separate from Jerusalem, though
standing on the same "mountain" as the great
fortress. If so, we might identify Jerusalem with
the city on Mount Zion, the Jebusite stronghold
of a later date, while "the city of Beth-Nin-ip"
would be that which centred round the temple
on Moriah.

However this may be, the fortress and the temple-
hill were distinct from one another in the days of
the Jebusites, and we may therefore assume that
they were also distinct in the age of Abraham.
This might explain why it was that the mountain
of Moriah on the summit of which the patriarch
offered his sacrifice was not enclosed within the
walls of Jerusalem, and was not covered with buildings. It was a spot, on the contrary, where sheep

could feed, and a ram be caught by its horns in the thick brushwood.

In entering Canaan, Abraham would have found himself still surrounded by all the signs of a familiar civilization. The long-continued influence and government of Babylonia had carried to "the land of the Amorites" all the elements of Chaldæan culture. Migration from Ur of the Chaldees to the distant West meant a change only in climate and population, not in the civilization to which the patriarch had been accustomed.

Even the Babylonian language was known and used in the cities of Canaan, and the literature of Babylonia was studied by the Canaanitish people. This is one of the facts which we have learnt from the discovery of the Tel el-Amarna tablets. The cuneiform system of writing and the Babylonian language had spread all over Western Asia, and nowhere had they taken deeper root than in Canaan. Here there were schools and teachers for instruction in the foreign language and script, and record-chambers and libraries in which the letters and books of clay could be copied and preserved.

Long before the discovery of the Tel el-Amarna tablets we might have gathered from the Old Testament itself that such libraries once existed in Canaan. One of the Canaanitish cities taken and destroyed by the Israelites was Debir in the mountainous part of Judah. But Debir, "the sanctuary," was also known by two other names.

It was called Kirjath-Sannah, "the city of Instruction," as well as Kirjath-Sepher, "the city of Books."

We now know, however, that the latter name is not quite correct. The Massoretic punctuation has to be emended, and we must read Kirjath-Sopher, "the city of the Scribe(s)," instead of Kirjath-Sepher, "the city of Book(s)." It is an Egyptian papyrus which has given us the exact name. In the time of Ramses II. an Egyptian scribe composed a sarcastic account of the misadventures met with by a tourist in Palestine— commonly known as *The Travels of a Mohar*— and in this mention is made of two adjoining towns in Southern Palestine called Kirjath-Anab and Beth-Sopher. In the Book of Joshua the towns of Anab and Kirjath-Sepher are similarly associated together, and it is plain, therefore, as Dr. W. Max Müller has remarked, that the Egyptian writer has interchanged the equivalent terms Kirjath, "city," and Beth, "house." He ought to have written Beth-Anab and Kirjath-Sopher. But he has given us the true form of the latter name, and as he has added to the word *Sopher* the determinative of "writing," he has further put beyond question the real meaning of the name. The city must have been one of those centres of Canaanitish learning, where, as in the libraries of Babylonia and Assyria, a large body of scribes was kept constantly at work.

The language employed in the cuneiform docu-

F

ments was almost always that of Babylonia, which had become the common speech of diplomacy and educated society. But at times the native language of the country was also employed, and one or two examples of it have been preserved. The legends and traditions of Babylonia served as text-books for the student, and doubtless Babylonian history was carried to the West as well. The account of Chedor-laomer's campaign might have been derived in this way from the clay-books of ancient Babylonia.

Babylonian theology, too, made its way to the West, and has left records of itself in the map of Canaan. In the names of Canaanitish towns and villages the names of Babylonian deities frequently recur. Rimmon or Hadad, the god of the air, whom the Syrians identified with the Sun-god, Nebo, the god of prophecy, the interpreter of the will of Bel-Merodach, Anu, the god of the sky, and Anat, his consort, all alike meet us in the names sometimes of places, sometimes of persons. Mr. Tomkins is probably right in seeing even in Beth-lehem the name of the primæval Chaldæan deity Lakhmu. The Canaanitish Moloch is the Babylonian Malik, and Dagon was one of the oldest of Chaldæan divinities and the associate of Anu. We have seen how ready Ebed-Tob was to identify the god he worshipped with the Babylonian Nin-ip, and among the Canaanites mentioned in the letters of Tel el-Amarna there is more than one whose name is compounded with that of a Babylonian god.

Writing and literature, religion and mythology, history and science, all these were brought to the peoples of Canaan in the train of Babylonian conquest and trade. Art naturally went hand in hand with this imported culture. The seal-cylinders of the Chaldæans were imitated, and Babylonian figures and ornamental designs were borrowed and modified by the Canaanitish artists. It was in this way that the rosette, the cherub, the sacred tree, and the palmette passed to the West, and there served to adorn the metal-work and pottery. New designs, unknown in Babylonia, began to develop ; among others, the heads of animals in gold and silver as covers for metal vases. Some of these "vases of Kaft," as they were called, are pictured on the Egyptian monuments, and Thothmes III. in his annals describes "the pateræ with goats' heads upon them and one with a lion's head, the productions of Zahi," or Palestine, which were brought to him as tribute.

The spoil which the same Pharaoh carried away from the Canaanitish princes gives us some idea of the art which they patronized. We hear of chariots and tent-poles covered with plates of gold, of iron armour and helmets, of gold and silver rings which were used in the place of money, of staves of ivory, ebony, and cedar inlaid with gold, of golden sceptres, of tables, chairs, and footstools of cedar wood, inlaid some of them with ivory, others with gold and precious stones, of vases and bowls of all kinds in gold, silver, and bronze, and of the two-handled cups which were a special manufacture of Phœnicia. Iron seems to have been worked in Canaan from an early date. The Israelites were unable to drive out the inhabitants of "the valley" because of their chariots of iron, and when the chariot of the Egyptian Mohar is disabled by the rough roads of the Canaanite mountains the writer of the papyrus already referred to makes him turn aside at once to a worker in iron. There was no difficulty in finding an ironsmith in Canaan.

The purple dye of Phœnicia had been famous from a remote antiquity. It was one of the chief objects of the trade which was carried on by the Canaanites with Egypt on the one side and Babylonia on the other. It was doubtless in exchange for the purple that the "goodly Babylonish garment" of which we are told in the Book of Joshua (vii. 21) made its way to the city of Jericho, for Babylonia was as celebrated for its embroidered robes as Canaan was for its purple dye.

We hear something about the trade of Canaan in one of the cuneiform tablets of Tel el-Amarna. This is a letter from Kallimma-Sin, king of Babylonia, to the Egyptian Pharaoh urging him to conclude a treaty in accordance with which the merchants of Babylonia might trade with Egypt on condition of their paying the customs at the frontier. Gold, silver, oil, and clothing are among the objects upon which the duty was to be levied. The frontier was probably fixed at the borders of the Egyptian province of Canaan rather than at those of Egypt itself.

Babylonia and the civilized lands of the East were not the only countries with which Canaanitish trade was carried on. Negro slaves were imported from the Soudan, copper and lead from Cyprus, and horses from Asia Minor, while the excavations of Mr. Bliss at Lachish have brought to light beads of Baltic amber mixed with the scarabs of the eighteenth Egyptian dynasty.

A large part of the trade of Phœnicia was carried on in ships. It was in this way that the logs of cedar were brought from the forests at the head of the Gulf of Antioch, and the purple murex from the coasts of the Ægean. Tyre, whose wealth is already celebrated in one of the Tel el-Amarna tablets, was built upon an island, and, as an Egyptian papyrus tells us, water had to be conveyed to it in boats. So, too, was Arvad, whose navy occupies an important place in the Tel el-Amarna correspondence. The ships of Canaan were, in fact, famous from an early date. Two classes of vessel known to the Egyptians were called "ships of Gebal" and "ships of Kaft," or Phœnicia, and Ebed-Tob asserts that "as long as a ship sails upon the sea, the arm (or oracle) of the Mighty King shall conquer the forces of Aram-Naharaim (Nahrima) and Babylonia." Balaam's prophecy—"Ships shall come from Chittim and shall afflict Asshur and shall afflict Eber," takes us back to the same age.

The Aram-Naharaim of Scripture is the Nahrina of the hieroglyphic texts, the Mitanni of the native inscriptions. The capital city Mitanni stood on the eastern bank of the Euphrates, at no great distance from Carchemish, but the Naharaim, or "Two Rivers," more probably mean the Euphrates and Orontes, than the Euphrates and Tigris. In one of the Tel el-Amarna tablets the country is called Nahrima, but its usual name is Mitanni or Mitanna. It was the first independent kingdom of any size or power on the frontiers of the Egyptian empire in the age of the eighteenth dynasty, and the Pharaohs Thothmes IV., Amenophis III., and Amenophis IV. successively married into its royal family.

The language of Mitanni has been revealed to us by the cuneiform correspondence from Tel el-Amarna. It was highly agglutinative, and unlike any other form of speech, ancient or modern, with which we are acquainted. Perhaps the speakers of it, like the Hittites, had descended from the north, and occupied territory which had originally belonged to Aramaic tribes. Perhaps, on the other hand, they represented the older population of the country which was overpowered and displaced by Semitic invaders. Which of these views is the more correct we shall probably never know.

Along with their own language the people of Mitanni had also their own theology. Tessupas was god of the atmosphere, the Hadad of the Semites, Sausbe was identified with the Phœnician

Ashteroth, and Sekhrus, Zizanu, and Zannukhu are mentioned among the other deities. But many of the divinities of Assyria were also borrowed—Sin the Moon-god, whose temple stood in the city of Harran, Ea the god of the waters, Bel, the Baal of the Canaanites, and Istar, "the lady of Nineveh." Even Amon the god of Thebes was adopted into the pantheon in the days of Egyptian influence.

How far back the interference of Aram-Naharaim in the affairs of Canaan may have reached it is impossible to say. But the kingdom lay on the high-road from Babylonia and Assyria to the West, and its rise may possibly have had something to do with the decline of Babylonian supremacy in Palestine. The district in which it grew up was called Suru or Suri by the Sumerian inhabitants of Chaldæa—a name which may be the origin of the modern "Syria," rather than Assyria, as is usually supposed, and the Semitic Babylonians gave it the title of Subari or Subartu. The conquest of Suri was the work of the last campaign of Sargon of Accad, and laid all northern Mesopotamia at his feet.

We gather from the letters of Tel el-Amarna that the Babylonians were still intriguing in Canaan in the century before the Exodus, though they acknowledged that it was an Egyptian province and subject to Egyptian laws. But the memory of the power they had once exercised there still survived, and the influence of their culture continued undiminished. When their rule actually ceased we do not yet know. It cannot have been very long, however, before the era of Egyptian conquest. In the Tel el-Amarna tablets they are always called Kassites, a name which could have been given to them only after the conquest of Babylonia by the Kassite mountaineers of Elam, and the rise of a Kassite dynasty of kings. This was about 1730 B.C. For some time subsequently, therefore, the government of Babylonia must still have been acknowledged in Canaan. With this agrees a statement of the Egyptian historian Manetho, upon which the critics, in their wisdom or their ignorance, have poured unmeasured contempt. He tells us that when the Hyksos were driven out of Egypt by Ahmes I., the founder of the eighteenth dynasty, they occupied Jerusalem and fortified it — not, as would naturally be imagined, against the Egyptian Pharaoh, but against "the Assyrians," as the Babylonians were called by Manetho's contemporaries. As long as there were no monuments to confront them the critics had little difficulty in proving that the statement was preposterous and unhistorical, that Jerusalem did not as yet exist, and that no Assyrians or Babylonians entered Palestine until centuries later. But we now know that Manetho was right and his critics wrong. Jerusalem did exist, and Babylonian armies threatened the independence of the Canaanite states. In one of his letters, Ebed-Tob, king of Jerusalem, tells the Pharaoh that he need not be alarmed about the Babylonians, for the temple at Jerusalem is strong enough to resist their attack. Rib-Hadad the governor of Gebal bears the same testimony. " When thou didst sit on the throne of thy father," he says, " the sons of Ebed-Asherah (the Amorite) attached themselves to the country of the Babylonians, and took the country of the Pharaoh for themselves; they (intrigued with) the king of Mitanna, and the king of the Babylonians, and the king of the Hittites." In another despatch he speaks in a similar strain : " The king of the Babylonians and the king of Mitanna are strong, and have taken the country of the Pharaoh for themselves already, and have seized the cities of thy governor." When George the Synkellos notes that the Chaldæans made war against the Phœnicians in B.C. 1556, he is doubtless quoting from some old and trustworthy source.

We must not imagine, however, that there was any permanent occupation of Canaan on the part of the Babylonians at this period of its history. It would seem rather that Babylonian authority was directly exercised only from time to time, and had to be enforced by repeated invasions and campaigns. It was the influence of Babylonian civilization and culture that was permanent, not the Babylonian government itself. Sometimes, indeed, Canaan became a Babylonian province, at other times there were only certain portions of the country which submitted to the foreign control, while again at other times the Babylonian rule was merely nominal. But it is clear that it was not until

Canaan had been thoroughly reduced by Egyptian arms that the old claim of Babylonia to be its mistress was finally renounced, and even then we see that intrigues were carried on with the Babylonians against the Egyptian authority.

It was during this period of Babylonian influence and tutelage that the traditions and myths of Chaldæa became known to the people of Canaan. It is again the tablets of Tel el-Amarna which have shown us how this came to pass. Among them are fragments of Babylonian legends, one of which endeavoured to account for the creation of man and the introduction of sin into the world, and these legends were used as exercise-books in the foreign language by the scribes of Canaan and Egypt who were learning the Babylonian language and script. If ever we discover the library of Kirjath-sepher we shall doubtless find among its clay records similar examples of Chaldæan literature. The resemblances between the cosmogonies of Phœnicia and Babylonia have often been pointed out, and since the discovery of the Chaldæan account of the Deluge by George Smith we have learned that between that account and the one which is preserved in Genesis there is the closest possible likeness, extending even to words and phrases. The long-continued literary influence of Babylonia in Palestine in the Patriarchal Age explains all this, and shows us how the traditions of Chaldæa made their way to the West. When Abraham entered Canaan, he entered a country whose educated inhabitants were already familiar with the books, the history, and the traditions of that in which he had been born. There were doubtless many to whom the name and history of " Ur of the Chaldees " were already known. It may even be that copies of the books in its library already existed in the libraries of Canaan.

There was one Babylonian hero at all events whose name had become so well known in the West that it had there passed into a proverb. This was the name of Nimrod, " the mighty hunter before the Lord." As yet the cuneiform documents are silent about him, but it is probable that he was one of the early Kassite kings who established their dominion over the cities of Babylonia. He is called the son of Cush or Kas, and " the beginning of his kingdom " was Babylon, which had now for six centuries been the capital of the country. His name, however, was as familiar to the Canaanite as it was to the inhabitant of Chaldæa, and the god before whom his exploits were displayed was Yahveh and not Bel.

It was about 1600 B.C. that the Hyksos were finally expelled from Egypt. They were originally Asiatic hordes who had overrun the valley of the Nile, and held it in subjection for several centuries. At first they had carried desolation with them wherever they went. The temples of the Egyptian gods were destroyed and their priests massacred. But before long Egyptian culture proved too strong for the invaders. The rude chief of a savage horde became transformed into an Egyptian Pharaoh, whose court resembled that of the ancient line of monarchs, and who surrounded himself with learned men. The cities and temples were restored and beautified, and art began to flourish once more. Except in one respect it became difficult to distinguish the Hyksos prince from his predecessors on the throne of Egypt. That one respect was religion. The supreme object of Hyksos worship continued to be Sutekh, the Baal of Western Asia, whose cult the foreigners had brought with them from their old homes. But even Sutekh was assimilated to Ra, the Sun-god of On, and the Hyksos Pharaohs felt no scruple in imitating the native kings and combining their own names with that of Ra. It was only the Egyptians who refused to admit the assimilation, and insisted on identifying Sutekh with Set the enemy of Horus.

At the outset all Egypt was compelled to submit to the Hyksos domination. Hyksos monuments have been found as far south as Gebelên and El-Kab, and the first Hyksos dynasty established its seat in Memphis, the old capital of the country. Gradually, however, the centre of Hyksos power retreated into the delta. Zoan or Tanis, the modern San, became the residence of the court : here the Hyksos kings were in close proximity to their kindred in Asia, and were, moreover, removed from the unmixed Egyptian population further south. From Zoan, "built"—or rather rebuilt—

"seven years" after Hebron (Num. xiii. 22), they governed the valley of the Nile. Their rule was assisted by the mutual jealousies and quarrels of the native feudal princes who shared between them the land of Egypt. The foreigner kept his hold upon the country by means of the old feudal aristocracy.

Thebes, however, had never forgotten that it had been the birthplace and capital of the powerful Pharaohs of the twelfth and thirteenth dynasties, of the mighty princes who had conquered the Soudan, and ruled with an iron hand over the feudal lords. The heirs of the Theban Pharaohs still survived as princes of Thebes, and behind the strong walls of El-Kab they began to think of independence. Apophis II. in his court at Zoan perceived the rising storm, and endeavoured to check it at its beginning. According to the story of a later day, he sent insulting messages to the prince of Thebes, and ordered him to worship Sutekh the Hyksos god. The prince defied his suzerain, and the war of independence began. It lasted for several generations, during which the Theban princes made themselves masters of Upper Egypt, and established a native dynasty of Pharaohs which reigned simultaneously with the Hyksos dynasty in the North.

Step by step the Hyksos stranger was pushed back to the north-eastern corner of the delta. At length Zoan itself fell into the hands of the Egyptians, and the Hyksos took refuge in the great fortress of Avaris on the extreme border of the kingdom. Here they were besieged by the Theban prince Ahmes, and eventually driven back to the Asia from which they had come. The eighteenth dynasty was founded, and Ahmes entered on that career of Asiatic conquest which converted Canaan into an Egyptian province. At first the war was one of revenge ; but it soon became one of conquest, and the war of independence was followed by the rise of the Egyptian empire. Thothmes II., the grandson of Ahmes, led his forces as far as the Euphrates and the land of Aram-Naharaim. The territories thus overrun in a sort of military reconnaissance were conquered and annexed by his son Thothmes III., during his long reign of fifty-four years (March 20, B.C. 1503 to February 14, B.C. 1449). Canaan on both sides of the Jordan was made into a province, and governed much as India is to-day. Some of the cities were allowed still to retain their old line of princes, who were called upon to furnish tribute to the Egyptian treasury and recruits to the Egyptian army. From time to time they were visited by an Egyptian "Commissioner," and an Egyptian garrison kept watch upon their conduct. Sometimes an Egyptian Resident was appointed by the side of the native king ; this was the case, for example, at Sidon and Hazor. Where, however, the city was of strategical or political importance it was incorporated into the Egyptian empire, and placed under the immediate control of an Egyptian governor, as at Megiddo, Gaza, Gebal, Gezer, and Tyre. Similarly

Ziri-Basana, " the field of Bashan," was under the government of a single *khazan* or " prefect." The troops, who also acted as police, were divided into various classes. There were the *tsabi yidati* or " auxiliaries," the *tsabi saruti* or " militia," the *Khabbati* or " Beduin plunderers," and the *tsabi matsarti* or " Egyptian soldiers of the garrison," as well as the *tsabi bitati* or " house-guards," who were summoned in cases of emergency. Among the auxiliaries were included the Serdani or Sardinians, while the Sute—the Sati or Sitti of the hieroglyphic texts—formed the larger portion of the Beduin (" Bashi-bazouks "), and the Egyptian forces were divided into the cavalry or rather charioteers, and the Misi (called Mas'u in the hieroglyphics) or infantry.

Fragments of the annals of Thothmes III. have been preserved on the shattered walls of his temple at Karnak. Here too we may read the lists of places he conquered in Palestine—the land of the Upper Lotan as it is termed—as well as in Northern Syria. Like the annals, the geographical lists have been compiled from memoranda made on the spot by the scribes who followed the army, and in some instances, at all events, it can be shown that they have been translated into Egyptian hieroglyphs from Babylonian cuneiform. The fact is an indication of the conquest that Asia was already beginning to make over her Egyptian conquerors. But the annals themselves are a further and still more convincing proof of Asiatic influence. To cover the walls of a temple with the history of campaigns in a foreign land, and an account of the tribute brought to the Pharaoh, was wholly contrary to Egyptian ideas. From the Egyptian point of view the decoration of the sacred edifice should have been theological only. The only subjects represented on it, so custom and belief had ruled, ought to be the gods, and the stereotyped phrases describing their attributes, their deeds, and their festivals. To substitute for this the records of secular history was Assyrian and not Egyptian. Indeed the very conception of annalistic chronicling, in which the history of a reign was given briefly year by year and campaign by campaign, belonged to the kingdoms of the Tigris and Euphrates, not to that of the Nile. It was a new thing in Egypt, and flourished there only during the short period of Asiatic influence. The Egyptian cared comparatively little for history, and made use of papyrus when he wished to record it. Unfortunately for us the annals of Thothmes III. remain the solitary monument of Egyptian chronicling on stone.

The twenty-second year of his reign (B.C. 1481) was that in which the Egyptian Pharaoh made his first determined effort to subdue Canaan. Gaza was occupied without much difficulty, and in the following year, on the fifth day of the month Pakhons, he set out from it, and eleven days later encamped at Ihem. There he learned that the confederated Canaanitish army, under the command of the king of Kadesh on the Orontes, was awaiting his attack at Megiddo. Not only were the various nations of Palestine represented in it, but contingents had come from Naharaim on the banks of the Euphrates, as well as from the Gulf of Antioch. For a while Thothmes hesitated whether to march against them by the road which led through 'Aluna to Taanach or by way of Zaft (perhaps Safed), whence he would have descended southward upon Megiddo. The arrival of his spies, however, determined him to take the first, and accordingly, after the officers had sworn that they would not leave their appointed posts in battle even to defend the person of the king, he started on his march, and on the nineteenth of the month pitched his tent at 'Aluna. The way had been rough and impassable for chariots, so that the king had been forced to march on foot.

'Aluna must have been close to Megiddo, since the rear of the Egyptian forces was stationed there during the battle that followed, while the southern wing extended to Taanach and the northern wing to Megiddo. The advanced guard pushed into the plain below, and the royal tent was set up on the bank of the brook of Qana, an affluent of the Kishon. The decisive struggle took place on the twenty-first of the month. Thothmes rode in a chariot of polished bronze, and posted himself among the troops on the north-west side of Megiddo. The Canaanites were unable to resist the Egyptian charge. They fled into the city, leaving behind them their horses and their chariots

G

plated with gold and silver, those who arrived after the gates of the town had been shut being drawn up over the walls by means of ropes. Had the Egyptians not stayed behind in order to plunder the enemy's camp they would have entered Megiddo along with the fugitives. As it was, they were compelled to blockade the city, building a rampart round it of "fresh green trees," and the besieged were finally starved into a surrender.

In the captured camp had been found the son of the king of Megiddo, besides a large amount of booty, including chariots of silver and gold from Asi or Cyprus. Two suits of iron armour were also obtained, one belonging to the king of Kadesh, the other to the king of Megiddo. The seven tent-poles of the royal tent, plated with gold, also fell into the hands of the Egyptians. The catalogue of the spoil was written down on a leather roll which was deposited in the temple of Amon at Thebes, and in it were enumerated: 3401 prisoners and 83 hands belonging to the slain, 32 chariots plated with gold, 892 ordinary chariots, 2041 mares, 191 foals, 602 bows, and 200 suits of armour.

Before the campaign was ended the Egyptian army had penetrated far to the north and captured Inuam, south of Damascus, as well as Anugas or Nukhasse, and Harankal, to the north of the land of the Amorites. All these places seem to have belonged to the king of Kadesh, as his property was carried away out of them. When Thothmes returned to Thebes the quantity of spoil be brought back with him was immense. " Besides precious stones," golden bowls, Phœnician cups with double handles and the like, there were 97 swords, 1784 pounds of gold rings and 966 pounds of silver rings, which served as money, a statue with a head of gold, tables, chairs, and staves of cedar and ebony inlaid with gold, ivory and precious stones, a golden plough, the golden sceptre of the conquered prince, and richly embroidered stuffs. The fields of the vanquished province were further measured by the Egyptian surveyors, and the amount of taxation annually due from them was fixed. More than 208,000 measures of wheat were moreover carried off to Egypt from the plain of Megiddo. The Canaanitish power was completely broken, and Thothmes was now free to extend his empire further to the north.

Accordingly in the following year (B.C. 1479) we find him receiving tribute from the Assyrian king. This consisted of leather bracelets, various kinds of wood, and chariots. It was probably at this time that Carchemish on the Euphrates was taken, the city being stormed from the riverside. Five years later the first part of the annals was engraved on the wall of the new temple of Amon at Karnak, and it concluded with an account of the campaign of the year. This had been undertaken in Northern Syria, and had resulted in the capture of Uarrt and Tunip, now Tennib, to the north-west of Aleppo. No less than one hundred pounds of silver and as many of gold were taken from Tunip, as well as lapis-lazuli from Babylonia, and malachite from the Sinaitic peninsula, together with vessels of iron and bronze. Some ships also were captured, laden with slaves, bronze, lead, white gold, and other products of the Greek seas. On the march home the Egyptian army took possession of Arvad, and seized its rich stores of wheat and wine. "Then the soldiers caroused and anointed themselves with oil as they used to do on feast days in the land of Egypt."

The next year Kadesh on the Orontes, near the Lake of Homs, was attacked and destroyed, its trees were cut down and its corn carried away. From Kadesh Thothmes proceeded to the land of Phœnicia, and took the cities of Zemar (now Sumra) and Arvad. The heirs of four of the conquered princes were carried as hostages to Egypt, "so that when one of these kings should die, then the Pharaoh should take his son and put him in his stead."

In B.C. 1472 the land of the Amorites was reduced, or rather that part of it which was known as Takhis, the Thahash of Genesis xxii. 24, on the shores of the Lake of Merna, in which we should probably see the Lake of Homs. Nearly 500 prisoners were led to Egypt. The Syrian princes now came to offer their gifts to the conqueror, bringing with them, among other things, more than 760 pounds of silver, 19 chariots covered with silver ornaments, and 41 leathern collars covered with bronze scales. At the same time the whole

country was thoroughly organized under the new
Egyptian administration.   Military roads were
constructed and provided with posting-houses, at
each of which relays of horses were kept in readi-
ness, as well as " the necessary provision of bread
of various sorts, oil, balsam, wine, honey, and fruits."
The quarries of the Lebanon were further required
to furnish the Pharaoh with limestone for his buildings in Egypt and elsewhere.

Two years later Thothmes was again in Syria.
He made his way as far as the Euphrates, and
there on the eastern bank erected a stele by the side
of one which his father Thothmes II. had already
set up.   The stele was an imperial boundary-stone
marking the frontier of the Egyptian empire.   It
was just such another stele that Hadad-ezer of
Zobah was intending to restore in the same place
when he was met and defeated by David (2 Sam.
viii. 3).

The Pharaoh now took ship and descended the
Euphrates, " conquering the towns and ploughing
up the fields of the king of Naharaim."   He then
re-ascended the stream to the city of Ni, where he
placed another stele, in proof that the boundary of
Egypt had been extended thus far.   Elephants
still existed in the neighbourhood, as they continued to do four and a half centuries later in
the time of the Assyrian king Tiglath-pileser I.
Thothmes amused himself by hunting them, and
no less than 120 were slain.

On his way home the tribute and "yearly tax"

of the inhabitants of the Lebanon was brought to
him, and the corvée-work annually required from
them was also fixed. Thothmes indulged his taste
for natural history by receiving as part of the
tribute various birds which were peculiar to Syria,
or at all events were unknown in Egypt, and
which, we are told, "were dearer to the king than
anything else." He had already established zoo-
logical and botanical gardens in Thebes, and the
strange animals and plants which his campaigns
furnished for them were depicted on the walls of
one of the chambers in the temple he built at
Karnak.

Before his return to Egypt he received the
tribute of "the king of Sangar," or Shinar, in
Mesopotamia, and "of the land of Khata the
greater." The first consisted for the most part of
lapis-lazuli, real and artificial, of which the most
prized was "the lapis-lazuli of Babylon." Among
the gifts was "a ram's head of real lapis-lazuli, 15
pounds in weight." The land of the Hittites, "the
greater," so called to distinguish it from the lesser
Hittite land in the south of Palestine, sent 8 rings
of silver, 400 pounds in weight, besides "a great
piece of crystal."

The following year Thothmes marched through
"the land of Zahi," the "dry land" of the Phœnician coast, to Northern Syria, where he punished the king of Anugas or Nukhasse, who
had shown symptoms of rebellion. Large quantities of gold and bronze were carried off, as

well as 15 chariots, plated with gold and silver, 6 iron tent-poles studded with precious stones, and 70 asses. Lead and various kinds of wood and stone, together with 608 jars of Lebanon wine, 2080 jars of oil, and 690 jars of balsam, were also received from Southern Syria, and posting-houses were established along the roads of the land of Zahi. A fleet of Phœnician merchant vessels was next sent to Egypt laden with logs of wood from the forests of Palestine and the Lebanon for the buildings of the king. At the same time, "the king of Cyprus," which now was an Egyptian possession, forwarded his tribute to the Pharaoh, consisting of 108 bricks of copper 2040 pounds in weight, 5 bricks of lead nearly 29,000 pounds in weight, 110 pounds of lapis-lazuli, an elephant's tusk, and other objects of value.

The next year (B.C. 1468) there was a campaign against the king of Naharaim, who had collected his soldiers and horses "from the extreme ends of the world." But the Mesopotamian army was utterly defeated. Its booty fell into the hands of the Egyptians, who, however, took only ten prisoners, which looks as if, after all, the battle was not on a very large scale.

In B.C. 1464 Thothmes was again in Northern Syria. Among the booty acquired during the expedition were "bowls with goats' heads on them, and one with a lion's head, the work of the land of Zahi." Horses, asses and oxen, 522 slaves, 156 jars of wine, 1752 jars of butter, 5 elephants' tusks,

2822 pounds of gold besides copper and lead, were
among the spoils of the campaign. The annual
tribute was only received from Cyprus, consisting
this time of copper and mares, as well as from
Aripakh, a district in the Taurus.

The next year the Pharaoh led his troops
against some country, the name of which is lost, in
" the land of the hostile Shasu" or Beduin. The
plunder which was carried off from it shows that it
was somewhere in Syria, probably in the region of
the Lebanon. Gold and silver, a silver double-
handled cup with a bull's head, iron, wine, balsam,
oil, butter and honey, were among the spoils of the
war. Tribute arrived also from " the king of the
greater Hittite land," which included a number of
negro slaves.

Revolt, however, now broke out in the north.
Tunip rebelled, as did also the king of Kadesh,
who built a " new" fortress to protect his city from
attack. Thothmes at once marched against them
by the road along " the coast," which led him
through the country of the Fenkhu or Phœnicians.
First he fell upon the towns of Alkana and utterly
destroyed them, and then poured his troops into
the neighbouring land of Tunip. The city of
Tunip was taken and burnt, its crops were trodden
under-foot, its trees cut down, and its inhabitants
carried into slavery. Then came the turn of
Kadesh. The " new" fortress fell at the first
assault, and the whole country was compelled to
submit.

The king of Assyria again sent presents to the Pharaoh which the Egyptian court regarded in the light of tribute. They consisted chiefly of large blocks of " real lapis-lazuli " as well as " lapis-lazuli of Babylon." More valuable gifts came from the subject princes of Syria. Foremost among these was " a king's daughter all glorious with [a vesture of] gold." Then there were four chariots plated with gold and six chariots of gold, iron armour inlaid with gold, a jug of silver, a golden helmet inlaid with lapis-lazuli, wine, honey and balsam, ivory and various kinds of wood, wheat in such quantities that it could not be measured, and the sixty-five slaves who had to be furnished each year as part of the annual tax.

The annals of the next two years are in too mutilated a condition to yield much information. Moreover, the campaigns carried on in them were mainly in the Soudan. In B.C. 1461 the record closes. It was in that year that the account of the Pharaoh's victories " which he had gained from the 23rd until the (4)2nd year "[1] were engraved upon the wall of the temple. And the chronicle con-cludes with the brief but expressive words, " Thus hath he done : may he live for ever ! "

Thothmes, indeed, did not live for ever, but he survived the completion of his temple fourteen years. His death was followed by the revolt of

[1] The inscription has " 32nd year," but as the wars extended beyond the 40th year of the king's reign this must be a sculptor's error.

Northern Syria, and the first achievement of his son and successor, Amenôphis II., was its suppression. Ni and Ugarit, the centres of disaffection, were captured and punished, and among the prisoners from Ugarit were 640 " Canaanite " merchants with their slaves. The name of Canaanite had thus already acquired that secondary meaning of " merchant " which we find in the Old Testament (Is. xxiii. 8 ; Ezek. xvii. 4). It is a significant proof of the commercial activity and trading establishments of the Canaanite race throughout the civilized world. Even a cuneiform tablet from Kappadokia, which is probably of the same age as the tablets of Tel el-Amarna, gives us the name of Kinanim " the Canaanite " as that of a witness to a deed. It was not always, however, that the Canaanites were so honourably distinguished. At times the name was equivalent to that of " slave " rather than of " merchant," as in a papyrus [1] where mention is made of Kan'amu or " Canaanite slaves from Khal." So too in another papyrus we hear of a slave called Saruraz the son of Naqati, whose mother was Kadi from the land of Arvad. The Egyptian wars in Palestine must necessarily have resulted in the enslavement of many of its inhabitants, and, as we have seen, a certain number of young slaves formed part of the annual tax levied upon Syria.

The successors of Thothmes III. extended the

---

[1] Anast. 4, 16, 2.

Egyptian empire far to the south in the Soudan. But its Asiatic limits had already been reached. Palestine, along with Phœnicia, the land of the Amorites and the country east of the Jordan, was constituted into an Egyptian province and kept strictly under Egyptian control. Further north the connection with the imperial government was looser. There were Egyptian fortresses and garrisons here and there, and certain important towns like Tunip near Aleppo and Qatna on the Khabûr were placed under Egyptian prefects. But elsewhere the conquered populations were allowed to remain under their native kings. In some instances, as, for example, in Anugas or Nukhasse, the kings were little more than satraps of the Pharaoh, but in other instances, like Alasiya, north of Hamath, they resembled the rulers of the protected states in modern India. In fact, the king of Alasiya calls the Pharaoh his "brother," and except for the obligation of paying tribute was practically an independent sovereign.

The Egyptian dominion was acknowledged as far north as Mount Amanus. Carchemish, soon to become a Hittite stronghold, was in Egyptian hands, and the Hittites themselves had not yet emerged from the fortresses of the Taurus. Their territory was still confined to Kataonia and Armenia Minor between Melitênê and the Saros, and they courted the favour of the Egyptian monarch by sending him gifts. Thothmes would have refused to believe that before many years were over they would wrest Northern Syria from his successors, and contend on equal terms with the Egyptian Pharaoh.

The Egyptian possessions on the east bank of Euphrates lay along the course of the Khabûr, towards the oasis of Singar or Shinar. North of the Belikh came the powerful kingdom of Mitanni, Aram-Naharaim as it is called in the Old Testament, which was never subdued by the Egyptian arms, and whose royal family intermarried with the successors of Thothmes. Mitanni, the capital, stood nearly opposite Carchemish, which thus protected the Egyptian frontier on the east.

Southward of the Belikh the frontier was formed by the desert. Syria, Bashan, Ammon, and Moab were all included in the Pharaoh's empire. But there it came to an end. Mount Seir was never conquered by the Egyptians. The "city" of Edom appears in one of the Tel el-Amarna tablets as a foreign state whose inhabitants wage war against the Egyptian territory. The conquest of the Edomites in their mountain fastnesses would have been a matter of difficulty, nor would anything have been gained by it. Edom was rich neither agriculturally nor commercially; it was, in fact, a land of barren mountains, and the trade which afterwards passed through the Arabah to Elath and Ezion-geber in the Gulf of Aqabah was already secured to the Egyptians through their possession of the Gulf of Suez. The first and last of the Pharaohs, so far as we know, who ventured on a

campaign against the wild tribes of Mount Seir,
was Ramses III. of the twentieth dynasty, and his
campaign was merely a punitive one.   No attempt
to incorporate the " Red Land " into his dominions
was ever made by an Egyptian king.

The Sinaitic peninsula, the province of Mafkat
or " Malachite," as it was called, had been in the
possession of the Egyptians since the time of
Zosir of the third dynasty, and it continued to be
regarded as part of the Egyptian kingdom up to
the age of the Ptolemies.   The earliest of Egyptian
rock-sculptures is engraved in the peninsula, and
represents Snefru, the founder of the fourth
dynasty, slaughtering the Beduin who inhabited it.
Its possession was valued on account of its mines
of copper and malachite.   These were worked by
the Egyptian kings with the help of convict
labour.   Garrisons were established to protect them
and the roads which led to them, colonies of
officials grew up at their side, and temples were
built dedicated to the deities of Egypt.   Even as
late as the reign of Ramses III. the amount of
minerals produced by the mines was enormous.
They existed for the most part on the western side
of the peninsula, opposite the Egyptian coast ; but
Ramses III. also opened copper mines in the land
of 'Ataka further east, and the name of the goddess
Hathor in hieroglyphics has been found by Dr.
Friedmann on the shores of Midian.

Vanquished Syria was made to contribute to the
endowments of the Egyptian temples.   Thus the

temple of Amon at Thebes was endowed by
Thothmes III. with the revenues of the three cities
Anugas, Inu'am, and Harankal; while Seti I., the
father of Ramses II., bestowed upon it "all the
silver, gold, lapis-lazuli, malachite, and precious
stones which he carried off from the humbled
land of Syria." Temples of the Egyptian gods, as
well as towns, were built in Syria itself; Meneptah
founded a city in the land of the Amorites;
Ramses III. erected a temple to Amon in "the
land of Canaan, great as the horizon of heaven
above, to which the people of Syria come with
their gifts"; and hieroglyphic inscriptions lately
discovered at Gaza show that another temple had
been built there by Amenophis II. to the goddess
Mut.

Amenophis had suppressed the rebellion in
Northern Syria with little trouble. Seven Amorite
kings were carried prisoners to Egypt from the
land of Takhis, and taken up the river as far as
Thebes. There six of them were hung outside the
walls of the city, as the body of Saul was hung by
the Philistines outside the walls of Beth-shan,
while the seventh was conveyed to Napata in
Ethiopia, and there punished in the same way in
order to impress a lesson of obedience upon the
negroes of the Soudan.

Amenophis II. was succeeded by Thothmes IV.,
who was called upon to face a new enemy, the
Hittites. It was at the commencement of his reign
that they first began to descend from their moun-

tain homes, and the frontier city of Tunip had to
bear the brunt of the attack. It was probably in
order to strengthen himself against these formidable
foes that the Pharaoh married the daughter of the
king of Mitanni, who changed her name to Mut-
em-ua. It was the beginning of those inter-
marriages with the princes of Asia which led to
the Asiatized court and religion of Amenophis IV.,
and finally to the overthrow of the eighteenth
dynasty.

The son of Mut-em-ua was Amenophis III.,
whose long reign of thirty-seven years was as
brilliant and successful as that of Thothmes III.
At Soleb between the second and third cataracts
he built a temple to his own deified self, and
engraved upon its columns the names of his vassal
states. Among them are Tunip and Kadesh,
Carchemish and Apphadana on the Khabûr. Sangar,
Assyria, Naharaim, and the Hittites also appear
among them, but this must be on the strength of
the tribute or presents which had been received
from them. The Pharaoh filled his harîm with
Asiatic princesses. His queen Teie, who exercised
an important influence upon both religion and
politics, came from Asia, and among his wives
were the sisters and daughters of the kings of
Babylonia and Mitanni, while one of his own
daughters was married to Burna-buryas the Babylonian sovereign. His marriage with Gilu-khipa,
the daughter of Sutarna, king of Aram-Naharaim,
was celebrated on a scarab, where it is further

related that she was accompanied to Egypt by three hundred and seventeen "maids of honour." Besides allying himself in marriage to the royal houses of Asia, Amenophis III. passed a good deal of his time in Syria and Mesopotamia, amusing himself with hunting lions. During the first ten years of his reign he boasts of having killed no less than one hundred and two of them. It was in the last of these years that he married queen Teie, who is said on scarabs to have been the daughter of "Yua and Tua." Possibly these are contracted forms of Tusratta and Yuni, who were at the time king and queen of Mitanni. But if so, it is curious that no royal titles are given to her parents ; moreover, the author of the scarabs has made Yua the father of the queen and Tua her mother. Tuya is the name of an Amorite in one of the Tel el-Amarna letters, while from another of them it would seem as if Teie had been the daughter of the Babylonian king. One of the daughters of Tusratta, Tadu-khipa, was indeed married to Amenophis, but she did not rank as chief queen. In the reign of Meneptah of the nineteenth dynasty the vizier was a native of Bashan, Ben-Mazana by name, whose father was called Yu the elder. Yua may therefore be a word of Amorite origin ; and a connection has been suggested between it and the Hebrew Yahveh. This, however, though possible, cannot be proved.

When Amenophis III. died his son Amenophis IV. seems to have been still a minor. At all events the queen-mother Teie became all-powerful in the government of the state. Her son, the new Pharaoh, had been brought up in the religious beliefs of his mother, and had inherited the ideas and tendencies of his Asiatic forefathers. A plaster-cast of his face, taken immediately after death, was discovered by Prof. Petrie at Tel el-Amarna, and it is the face of a refined and thoughtful theorist, of a philosopher rather than of a king, earnest in his convictions almost to fanaticism.

Amenophis IV. undertook no less a task than that of reforming the State religion of Egypt. For many centuries the religion of the priests and scribes had been inclining to pantheism. Inside the temples there had been an esoteric teaching, that the various deities of Egypt were but manifestations of the one supreme God. But it had hardly passed outside them. With the accession of Amenophis IV. to the throne came a change. The young king boldly rejected the religion of which he was officially the head, and professed himself a worshipper of the one God whose visible semblance was the solar disk. Alone of the deities of Egypt Ra, the ancient Sun-god of Heliopolis, was acknowledged to be the representative of the true God. It was the Baal-worship of Syria, modified by the philosophic conceptions of Egypt. The Aten-Ra of the "heretic" Pharaoh was an Asiatic Baal, but unlike the Baal of Canaan he stood alone; there were no other Baals, no Baalim, by the side of him.

H

Amenophis was not content with preaching and encouraging the new faith ; he sought to force it upon his subjects. The other gods of Egypt were proscribed, and the name and head of Amon, the patron god of Thebes, to whom his ancestors had ascribed their power and victories, were erased from the monuments wherever they occurred. Even his own father's name was not spared, and the emissaries of the king, from one end of the country to the other, defaced that portion of it which contained the name of the god. His own name was next changed, and Amenophis IV. became Khu-n-Aten, " the splendour of the solar disk."

Khu-n-Aten's attempt to overthrow the ancient faith of Egypt was naturally resisted by the powerful priesthood of Thebes. A religious war was declared for the first time, so far as we know, in the history of mankind. On the one side a fierce persecution was directed against the adherents of the old creed ; on the other side every effort was made to impede and defeat the Pharaoh. His position grew daily more insecure, and at last he turned his back on the capital of his fathers, and built himself a new city far away to the north. The priests of Amon had thus far triumphed ; the old idolatrous worship was carried on once more in the great temple of Karnak, though its official head was absent, and Khu-n-Aten with his archives and his court had fled to a safer home. Upper Egypt was left to its worship of Amon and Min, while the king established himself nearer his Canaanite possessions.

Here on the eastern bank of the Nile, about midway between Minyeh and Siût, the new capital was founded on a strip of land protected from attack by a semi-amphitheatre of cliffs. The city, with its palaces and gardens, extended nearly two miles in length along the river bank. In its midst rose the temple of the new god of Egypt, and hard by the palace of the king. Both were brilliant with painting and sculpture, and inlaid work in precious stones and gold. Even the floors were frescoed, while the walls and columns were enamelled or adorned with the most costly materials that the Egyptian world could produce. Here and there were statues of alabaster, of bronze or of gold, some of them almost Greek in form and design. Along with the reform in religion there had gone a reform in art. The old conventionalized art of Egypt was abandoned, and a new art had been introduced which aimed at imitating nature with realistic fidelity.

The mounds which mark the site of Khu-n-Aten's city are now known as Tel el-Amarna. It had a brief but brilliant existence of about thirty years. Then the enemies of the Pharaoh and his work of reform finally prevailed, and his city with its temple and palaces was levelled to the ground. It is from among its ruins that the wondering fellah and explorer of to-day exhume the gorgeous relics of its past.

But among these relics none have proved more precious than the clay tablets inscribed with cuneiform characters, which have revolutionized our conceptions of the ancient East. They were preserved in the Foreign Office of the day. This formed part of the public buildings connected with the palace, and the bricks of which it was built were stamped with an inscription describing its character. Many of the tablets had been brought from the archive chamber of Thebes, but the greater part of the collection belongs to the reign of Khu-n-Aten himself. It consists almost entirely of official correspondence ; of letters from the kings of Babylonia and Assyria, of Mesopotamia and Kappadokia, and of despatches from the Egyptian governors and vassal-princes in Syria and Palestine. They furnish us with a living and unexpected picture of Canaan about 1400 B.C.

Fragments of dictionaries for the use of the scribes have also been recovered from the *débris* of the building, as well as the seal of a servant of Samas-akh-iddin who looked after the cuneiform correspondence. Like several of the Canaanitish governors, he bore a Babylonian name. Even the brother of Amenophis III., who had been made king of Nukhasse, had received the Babylonian name of Rimmon-nirari. No stronger proof could be found of the extent and strength of Babylonian influence in the West.

At Khut-Aten, as the " heretic " Pharaoh called his new capital, he was surrounded by the adherents of the new faith. Many of them were doubtless Egyptians, but many, perhaps the majority, were

of Asiatic extraction.   Already under his father
and grandfather the court had been filled with
Canaanites and other natives of Asia, and the great
offices of state had been occupied by them.   Now
under Khu-n-Aten the Asiatic character of the
government was increased tenfold.   The native
Egyptian had to make way for the foreigner, and
the rule of the Syrian stranger which seemed to
have been expelled with the Hyksos was restored
under another form.   Canaan was nominally a
subject province of Egypt, but in reality it had led
its conqueror captive.   A semi-Asiatic Pharaoh
was endeavouring to force an Asiatic form of faith
upon his subjects, and entrusting his government to
Asiatic officials ; even art had ceased to be
Egyptian and had put on an Asiatic dress.

The tombs of Khu-n-Aten's followers are cut
in the cliffs at the back of the city, while his own
sepulchre is towards the end of a long ravine which
runs out into the eastern desert between two
lofty lines of precipitous rock.   But few of them
are finished, and the sepulchre of the king himself,
magnificent in its design, is incomplete and
mutilated.   The sculptures on the walls have been
broken, and the granite sarcophagus in which the
body of the great king rested has been shattered
into fragments before it could be lifted into the
niche where it was intended to stand.   The royal
mummy was torn into shreds, and the porcelain
figures buried with it dashed to the ground.

It is clear that the death of Khu-n-Aten must

have been quickly followed by the triumph of his enemies. His capital was overthrown, the stones of its temple carried away to Thebes, there to adorn the sanctuary of the victorious Amon, and the adherents of his reform either slain or driven into exile. The vengeance executed upon them was national as well as religious. It meant not only a restoration of the national faith, but also the restoration of the native Egyptian to the government of his country. The feelings which inspired it were similar to those which underlay the movement of Arabi in our own time, and there was no English army to stand in the way of its success. The rise of the nineteenth dynasty represents the triumph of the national cause.

The cuneiform letters of Tel el-Amarna show that already before Khu-n-Aten's death his empire and power were breaking up. Letter after letter is sent to him from the governors in Canaan with urgent requests for troops. The Hittites were attacking the empire in the north, and rebels were overthrowing it within. " If auxiliaries come this year," writes Ebed-Tob of Jerusalem, "the provinces of the king my lord will be preserved ; but if no auxiliaries come the provinces of the king my lord will be destroyed." To these entreaties no answer could be returned. There was civil and religious war in Egypt itself, and the army was needed to defend the Pharaoh at home.

The picture of Canaan presented to us by the Tel el-Amarna correspondence has been supple-

mented by the discovery of Lachish.   Five years
ago Prof. Flinders Petrie undertook to excavate
for the Palestine Exploration Fund in the lofty
mound of Tel el-Hesi in Southern Palestine.   Tel
el-Hesi stands midway between Gaza and Hebron
on the edge of the Judæan mountains, and over-
looking a torrent stream.   His excavations resulted
in the discovery of successive cities built one upon
the ruins of the other, and in the probability that
the site was that of Lachish.   The excavations were
resumed by Mr. Bliss in the following year, and
the probability was raised to practical certainty.
The lowest of the cities was the Lachish of the
Amorite period, whose crude brick walls, nearly
twenty-nine feet in thickness, have been brought to
light, while its pottery has revealed to us for the first
time the characteristics of Amorite manufacture.
The huge walls bear out the testimony of the
Israelitish spies, that the cities of the Amorites
were "great and walled up to heaven" (Deut. i. 28).
They give indications, however, that in spite of
their strength the fortresses they enclosed must have
been captured more than once.   Doubtless this was
during the age of the Egyptian wars in Canaan.

As at Troy, it is probable that it was only the
citadel which was thus strongly fortified.   Below
it was the main part of the town, the inhabitants
of which took refuge in the citadel when an enemy
threatened to attack them.   The fortified part,
indeed, was not of very large extent.   Its ruins
measured only about two hundred feet each way,

while the enclosure within which it stands is a
quarter of a mile in diameter. Here a regular series
of pottery has been found, dating from the post-
exilic age through successive strata back to the
primitive Amoritish fortress. To Prof. Petrie belongs the credit of determining the characteristics
of these various strata, and fixing their approxi-
mate age.

The work begun by Prof. Petrie was continued
by Mr. Bliss. Deep down among the ruins of the
Amoritish town he found objects which take us
back to the time of Khu-n-Aten and his predecessors. They consist of Egyptian beads and
scarabs of the eighteenth dynasty, and on one of
the beads are the name and title of " the royal wife
Teie." Along with them were discovered beads of
amber which came from the Baltic as well as seal-
cylinders, some of them imported from Babylonia,
others western imitations of Babylonian work.
The Babylonian cylinders belong to the period
which extends from 3000 to 1500 B.C., while the
imitations are similar in style to those which have
been found in the pre-historic tombs of Cyprus and
Phœnicia.

But there was one discovery made by Mr. Bliss
which far surpasses in interest all the rest. It is
that of a cuneiform tablet, similar in character, in
contents, and in age to those which have come
from Tel el-Amarna. Even the Egyptian governor
mentioned in it was already known to us from the
Tel el-Amarna correspondence as the governor of

Lachish. One of the cuneiform letters now preserved at Berlin was written by him, and Ebed-
Tob informs us that he was subsequently murdered
by the people of his own city.

Here is a translation of the letter discovered at
Tel el-Hesi [1] :—

"To . . rabbat (?) [or perhaps : To the officer
Baya] (thus speaks) . . abi. At thy feet I prostrate myself. Verily thou knowest that Dan-
Hadad and Zimrida have inspected the whole of
the city, and Dan-Hadad says to Zimrida : Send
Yisyara to me [and] give me 3 shields (?) and 3
slings and 3 falchions, since I am prefect (?) over
the country of the king and it has acted against
me ; and now I will restore thy possession which
the enemy took from thee ; and I have sent my
. . . , and . . . rabi-ilu . . . has despatched his
brother [with] these words."

Yisyara was the name of an Amorite, as we learn
from one of the Tel el-Amarna tablets, where he is
mentioned along with other rebels as being sent in
fetters of bronze to the king. Of Dan-Hadad we
know nothing further, but Zimrida's letter is as
follows :—

"To the king my lord, my god, my Sun-god,

[1] This translation differs in some respects from that
previously given by me, as it is based on the copy of the
text made from the original at Constantinople by Dr. Scheil
(*Recueil de Travaux relatifs à la Philologie et à l'Archéologie
égyptiennes et assyriennes*, xv. 3, 4, 137). As I stated at the
time, my copy was made from a cast and was therefore uncertain in several places. I am doubtful whether even now
the published text is correct throughout.

the Sun-god who is from heaven, thus (writes)
Zimridi, the governor of the city of Lachish. Thy
servant, the dust of thy feet, at the feet of the king
my lord, the Sun-god from heaven, bows himself
seven times seven. I have very diligently listened
to the words of the messenger whom the king my
lord has sent to me, and now I have despatched (a
mission) according to his message."

It was towards the end of Khu-n-Aten's reign,
when the Egyptian empire was falling to pieces,
that the murder of Zimrida took place. Ebed-Tob
thus describes it in a letter to the secretary of the
Pharaoh : " The Khabiri (or Confederates) are
capturing the fortresses of the king. Not a single
governor remains among them to the king my
lord ; all are destroyed. Behold, Turbazu thy
officer [has fallen] in the great gate of the city of
Zelah. Behold, the servants who acted against the
king have slain Zimrida of Lachish. They have
murdered Jephthah-Hadad thy officer in the gate
of the city of Zelah."

We hear of another governor of Lachish, Yabni-el
by name, but he probably held office before
Zimrida. At all events the following despatch of
his has been preserved :—

"To the king my lord, my god, my Sun-god,
the Sun-god who is from heaven, thus (writes)
Yabni-el, the governor of the city of Lachish, thy
servant, the dust of thy feet, the groom of thy
horses ; at the feet of the king my lord, my god,
my Sun-god, the Sun-god who is from heaven,

seven times seven I bow myself. Glorious and
supreme [art thou]. I the groom of [the horses]
of the king my lord, listen to the [words] of the
king my lord. Now have I heard all the words
which Baya the prefect has spoken to me. Now
have I done everything."

Zimrida of Lachish must be distinguished from
another Canaanite of the same name who was
governor of Sidon. This latter was a personal
enemy of Rib-Hadad the governor of Gebal, whose
letters to Khu-n-Aten form a considerable portion
of the Tel el-Amarna collection. The authority of
Rib-Hadad originally extended over the greater
part of Phœnicia, and included the strong fortress
of Zemar or Simyra in the mountains. One by
one, however, his cities were taken from him by
his adversaries whom he accuses of rebellion against
the Pharaoh. His letters to Egypt are accordingly
filled with imploring appeals for help. But none
was sent, and as his enemies equally professed their
loyalty to the Egyptian government, it is doubtful
whether this was because the Pharaoh suspected
Rib-Hadad himself of disaffection or because no
troops could be spared.

Rib-Hadad had been appointed to his post by
Amenophis III., and in one of his letters he looks
back regretfully on "the good old times." When
his letters were written he was old and sick.
Abimelech, the governor of Tyre, was almost the
only friend who remained to him. Not content
with fomenting rebellion in his district, and taking

his cities from him, his enemies accused him to the Pharaoh of disloyalty and misdoing. Those accusations were in some cases founded on truth. He confesses to having fled from his city, but he urges that it was to save his life. The troops he had begged for had not been sent to him, and he could no longer defend either his city or himself. He also alleges that the excesses committed by some of his servants had been without his knowledge. This seems to have been in answer to a despatch of Ammunira, the prefect of Beyrout, in which he informed the king that he was keeping the brother of the governor of Gebal as a hostage, and that the latter had been intriguing against the government in the land of the Amorites.

Chief among the adversaries of Rib-Hadad was Ebed-Asherah, a native of the land of Barbarti, and the governor of the Amoritish territory. Several of his sons are mentioned, but the ablest and most influential of them was Aziru or Ezer, who possessed a considerable amount of power. The whole family, while professing to be the obedient servants of the Pharaoh, nevertheless acted with a good deal of independence, and sought to aggrandise themselves at the expense of the neighbouring governors. They had at their disposal a large body of " plunderers," or Beduin from the eastern desert, and Rib-Hadad accuses them of forming secret alliances with the kings of Babylonia, of Mitanni and of the Hittites. The authority of Aziru extended to the northern frontier of the empire; we find him sent with the Egyptian general Khatip, or Hotep, to oppose the Hittite invasion, and writing to the king as well as to the prime minister Dudu to explain why they had not succeeded in doing so. Tunip had been invested by the enemy, and Aziru fears that it may fall into their hands. The Hittites had already made their way into the land of Nukhasse, and were from thence marching up into the land of the Amorites.

On the heels of these despatches came a long letter from the people of Tunip, complaining of the conduct of Aziru, and protesting against his doing to them what he had done to the city of Ni. He was at the time in the land of the Hittites, doubtless carrying on the war against the general enemy.

To these accusations Aziru made a full reply. "O my lord," he begins, "hearken not to the wicked men who slander me before the king my lord : I am thy servant for ever." He had been charged with want of respect to the Pharaoh, on the ground that he had not received the royal commissioner Khani on his arrival at Tunip. But, he replies, he did not know that the commissioner was coming, and as soon as he heard that he was on the road he "followed him, but failed to overtake him." In his absence Khani was duly received by the brethren of Aziru, and Belti-el (or Bethuel) furnished him with meat and bread and wine. Moreover, on his way home he was met by Aziru himself, who provided the commissioner with horses and mules. A more serious charge was that of seizing the city of Zemar. To this Aziru answers that it was done in self-defence, as the kings of Nukhasse had always been hostile to him, and had robbed him of his cities at the instigation of Khatip, who had also carried away all the silver and gold which the king had placed under his care. Moreover he had not really seized Zemar, but had won the people over to himself by means of gifts. Lastly, he denied the accusation that he had received the envoy of the king of the Hittites and refused to receive the Egyptian messenger, although the country he governed belonged to the king, and the king had appointed him over it. Let the Egyptian envoy make inquiries, he urges, and he will find that Aziru has acted uprightly.

The capture of Zemar forms the burden of many of the letters of Rib-Hadad. It had been besieged for two months by Ebed-Asherah, who had vainly attempted to corrupt the loyalty of the governor of Gebal. For the time Rib-Hadad managed to save the city, but Aziru allied himself with Arvad and the neighbouring towns of Northern Phœnicia, captured twelve of Rib-Hadad's men, demanded a ransom of fifty pieces of silver for each of them, and seized the ships of Zemar, Beyrout, and Sidon. The forces sent from Gebal to Zemar were made prisoners by the Amorite chief at Abiliya, and the position of Rib-Hadad daily became more desperate. Pa-Hor, the Egyptian governor of Kumidi, joined his opponents, and induced the Sute or Beduin to attack his Sardinian guards. Yapa-Hadad, another governor, followed the example of Pa-Hor, and Zimridi the governor of Sidon had from the first been his enemy. Tyre alone remained faithful to his cause, though an " Ionian " who had been sent there on a mission from Egypt had handed over horses, chariots, and men to Ebed-Asherah, and it was accordingly to Tyre that Rib-Hadad sent his family for safety. Tyre, however, now began to suffer like Gebal in consequence of the alliance between Zimridi and Ebed-Asherah.

Zemar eventually fell into the hands of Ebed-Asherah and his sons, its prefect Khayapa or Khaip being slain during the assault. Abimelech, the governor of Tyre, accuses Zimridi of having been the cause. Whether this were so or not, it placed the whole of Northern Phœnicia under the government or the influence of the Amorite chiefs. If Rib-Hadad spoke the truth, Ebed-Asherah had " sent to the soldiers in Bit-Ninip, saying, ' Gather yourselves together, and let us march up against Gebal, if therein are any who have saved themselves from our hands, and we will appoint governors throughout all the provinces ; ' so all the provinces went over to the Beduin." Provisions began to be scarce in Gebal, and the governor writes to Egypt for corn.

Rib-Hadad now threatened the Pharaoh with deserting to his enemies if succour was not forthcoming immediately, and at the same time he appealed to Amon-apt and Khayapa, the Egyptian commissioners who had been sent to inquire into the condition of affairs in Canaan. The appeal was so far successful that troops were despatched to Zemar. But it was too late: along with Arka it had already been occupied by Ebed-Asherah, who thereupon writes to the Pharaoh, protesting his loyalty to Khu-n-Aten, declaring that he is "the house-dog" of the king, and that he guards the land of the Amorites for "the king" his lord. He further calls on the Egyptian commissioner Pakhanate, who had been ordered to visit him, to bear witness that he was "defending" Zemar and its fields for the king. That Pakhanate was friendly to Ebed-Asherah may be gathered from a despatch of Rib-Hadad, in which he accuses that officer of refusing to send any troops to the relief of Gebal, and of looking on while Zemar fell. Ebed-Asherah goes on to beg the king to come himself, and see with his own eyes how faithful a governor he really was.

The letters of Abimelech of Tyre told a different tale, and the unfortunate Pharaoh might well be excused if he was as much puzzled as we are to know on which side the truth lay, or whether indeed it lay on either. Abimelech had a grievance of his own. As soon as Zimridi of Sidon learned that he had been appointed governor of Tyre, he seized the neighbouring city of Usu, which seems to have occupied the site of Palætyros on the mainland, thereby depriving the Tyrians of their supplies of wood, food, and fresh water. The city of Tyre was at the time confined to a rocky island, to which provisions and water had to be conveyed in boats. Hence the hostile occupation of the town on the mainland caused many of its inhabitants to die of want. To add to their difficulties, the city was blockaded by the combined fleet of Sidon, Arvad, and Aziru. Ilgi, "king of Sidon," seems to have fled to Tyre for protection, while Abimelech reports that the king of Hazor had joined the Beduin under Ebed-Asherah and his sons. It may be noted that a letter of this very king of Hazor has been preserved, as well as another from Ebed-Sullim, the Egyptian governor of the city, whose powers were co-extensive with those of the king.

Soon afterwards, however, the Sidonian ships were compelled to retreat, and the Tyrian governor made ready to pursue them. Meanwhile he sent his messenger Elimelech to Khu-n-Aten with various presents, and gave the king an account of what had been happening in "Canaan." The Hittite troops had departed, but Etagama—elsewhere called Aidhu-gama—the *pa-ur* or "prince" of Kadesh, in the land of Kinza, had joined Aziru in attacking Namya-yitsa, the governor of Kumidi. Abimelech adds that his rival Zimridi of Sidon had collected ships and men from the cities of Aziru against him, and had consequently defeated him, but if the Pharaoh would send only four companies of troops to his rescue all would be well.

I

Zimridi, however, was not behindhand in forwarding his version of events to the Egyptian court, and assuring the king of his unswerving fidelity. "Verily the king my lord knows," he says, "that the queen of the city of Sidon is the handmaid of the king my lord, who has given her into my hand, and that I have hearkened to the words of the king my lord that he would send to his servant, and my heart rejoiced and my head was exalted, and my eyes were enlightened, and my ears heard the words of the king my lord. . . And the king my lord knows that hostility is very strong against me ; all the [fortresses] which the king gave into [my hand] had revolted" to the Beduin, but had been retaken by the commander of the Egyptian forces. The letter throws a wholly different light on the relations of the two rival parties in Phœnicia.

The assertions of Rib-Hadad, however, are supported by those of his successor in the government of Gebal, El-rabi-Hor. Rib-Hadad himself disappears from the scene. He may have died, for he complains that he is old and sick ; he may have been driven out of Gebal, for in one of his despatches he states that the city was inclined to revolt, while in another he tells us that even his own brother had turned against him and gone over to the Amorite faction. Or he may have been displaced from his post ; at all events, we hear that the Pharaoh had written to him, saying that Gebal was rebellious, and that there was a large amount of royal property in it. We hear also that Rib-Hadad had sent his son to the Egyptian court to plead his cause there, alleging age and infirmities as a reason for not going himself. However- it may have been, we find a new governor in Gebal, who bears the hybrid name of El-rabi-Hor, "a great god is Horus."

His first letter is to protest against Khu-n-Aten's mistrust of Gebal, which he calls "thy city and the city of [thy] fathers," and to assert roundly that "Aziru is in rebellion against the king my lord." Aziru had made a league(?) with the kings of Ni, Arvad, and Ammiya (the Beni-Ammo of Num. xxii. 5),[1] and with the help of the Amorite Palasa was destroying the cities of the Pharaoh. So El-rabi-Hor asks the king not to heed anything the rebel may write about his seizure of Zemar or his massacre of the royal governors, but to send some troops to himself for the defence of Gebal. In a second letter he reiterates his charges against Aziru, who had now "smitten" Adon, the king of Arka, and possessed himself of Zemar and the other towns of Phœnicia, so that Gebal "alone" is on the side of the king, who "looks on" without doing anything. Moreover a fresh enemy had arisen in the person of Eta-gama of Kadesh, who had joined himself with the king of the Hittites and the king of Naharaim.

Letters to Khu-n-Aten from Akizzi the governor of Qatna, which, as we learn from the inscriptions

---

[1] See above, p. 64.

of Assur-natsir-pal, was situated on the Khabûr, represent Aziru in the same light. First of all, the Egyptian government is informed that the king of the Hittites, together with Aidhu-gama (or Eta-gama) of Kadesh has been invading the Egyptian territory, burning its cities, and carrying away from Qatna the image of the Sun-god. Khu-n-aten, it is urged, could not allow the latter crime to go un-punished. The Sun-god had created him and his father, and had caused them to be called after his own name. He was the supreme object of the Pharaoh's worship, the deity for whose sake Khu-n-Aten had deserted Thebes.

The Hittite king had been joined in his invasion of Syria by the governors of some otherwise un-known northern cities, but the kings of Nukhasse, Ni, Zinzar (the Sonzar of the Egyptian texts), and Kinanat (the Kanneh of Ezek. xxvii. 23) remained faithful to the Egyptian monarch. The rebel governors, however, were in the land of Ube,—the Aup of the hieroglyphics,—which they were urging Aidhu-gama to invade.

Another letter brings Aziru upon the scene. He is accused of having invaded the land of Nukhasse, and made prisoners of the people of Qatna. The Pharaoh is prayed to rescue or ransom them, and to send chariots and soldiers to the help of his Meso-potamian subjects. If they come all the lands round about will acknowledge him as lord, and he will be lord also of Nukhasse ; if they do not come, the men of Qatna will be forced to obey Aziru.

It is probable that the misdeeds of Aziru which are here referred to were committed at the time he was in Tunip, professedly protecting it against Hittite attack. It would seem from what Akizzi says, that instead of faithfully performing his mission, he had aimed at establishing his own power in Northern Syria. While nominally an officer of the Pharaoh, he was really seeking to found an Amorite kingdom in the north. In this he would have been a predecessor of Og and Sihon, whose kingdoms were built up on the ruins of the Egyptian empire.

A despatch, however, from Namya-yitsa, the governor of Kumidi, sets the conduct of Aziru in a more favourable light. It was written at a somewhat later time, when rebellion against the Egyptian authority was spreading throughout Syria. A certain Biridasyi had stirred up the city of Inu'am, and after shutting its gate upon Namya-yitsa had entered the city of Ashtaroth-Karnaim in Bashan, and there seized the chariots belonging to the Pharaoh, handing them over to the Beduin. He then joined the kings of Buzruna (now Bosra) and Khalunni (near the Wadi 'Allân), in a plot to murder Namya-yitsa, who escaped, however, to Damascus, though his own brothers turned against him. The rebels next attacked Aziru, captured some of his soldiers, and in league with Etu-gama wasted the district of Abitu. Etakkama, however, as Etu-gama spells his own name, professed to be a loyal servant of the Egyptian king, and one of the Tel el-Amarna letters is from him.

We next hear of Namya-yitsa in Accho or Acre, where he had taken refuge with Suta, or Seti, the Egyptian commissioner. Seti had already been in Jerusalem, and had been inquiring there into the behaviour of Ebed-Tob.

The picture of incipient anarchy and rebellion which is set before us by the correspondence from Phœnicia and Syria is repeated in that from the centre and south of Palestine. In the centre the chief seats of the Egyptian government were at Megiddo, at Khazi (the Gaza of 1 Chron. vii. 28), near Shechem, and at Gezer. Each of these towns was under an Egyptian governor, specially appointed by the Pharaoh.

The governor of Khazi bore the name of Su-yarzana, Megiddo was under the authority of Biridî, while the governor of Gaza was Yapakhi. There are several letters in the Tel el-Amarna collection from the latter official, chiefly occupied with demands for help against his enemies. The district under his control was attacked by the Sute or Beduin, led by a certain Labai or Labaya and his sons. Labai, though of Beduin origin, was himself professedly an Egyptian official, the Egyptian policy having been to give the title of governor to the powerful Beduin sheikhs, and to attach them to the Egyptian government by the combined influence of bribery and fear. Labai accordingly writes to the Pharaoh to defend himself against the charges that had been brought against him, and to assure Khu-n-Aten that he was "a faithful servant of the king"; "I have not sinned, and I have not offended, and I do not withhold my tribute or neglect the command to turn back my officers." Labai, it would seem, had been appointed by Amenophis III. governor of Shunem and Beneberak (Joshua xix. 45), and had captured the city of Gath-Rimmon when it revolted against the Pharaoh; but after the death of Amenophis he and his two sons had attacked the Egyptian officials in true Beduin style, and had taken every opportunity of pillaging central and Southern Palestine. As we shall see, Labai and his ally, Malchiel, were among the chief adversaries of Ebed-Tob of Jerusalem.

On one occasion, however, Labai was actually made prisoner by one of the Egyptian officers. There is a letter from Biridî stating that Megiddo was threatened by Labai, and that although the garrison had been strengthened by the arrival of some Egyptian troops, it was impossible to venture outside the gates of the town for fear of the enemy, and that unless two more regiments were sent the city itself was likely to fall. Whether the additional forces were sent or not we do not know. Labai, however, had to fly for his life along with his confederate Yasdata, who was the governor of some city near Megiddo, as we learn from a letter of his in which he speaks of being with Biridî. Of Yasdata we hear nothing further, but Labai was captured in Megiddo by Zurata, the prefect of Acre, who, under the pretext that he was going to send his prisoner in a ship to Egypt, took him first to the town of Khinatuna ('En'athôn), and then to his own house, where he was induced by a bribe to set him free along with his companion, Hadad-mekhir (who, by the way, has bequeathed to us two letters).

It was probably after this that Labai wrote to the Pharaoh to exculpate himself, though his language, in spite of its conventional submissiveness, could not have been very acceptable at the Egyptian court. In one of his letters he excuses himself partly on the ground that even "the food of his stomach" had been taken from him, partly that he had attacked and entered Gezer only in order to recover the property of himself and his friend Malchiel, partly because a certain Bin-sumya whom the Pharaoh had sent against him had really "given a city and property in it to my father, saying that if the king sends for my wife I shall withhold her, and if the king sends for myself I shall give him instead a bar of copper in a large bowl and take the oath of allegiance." A second letter is still more uncompromising. In this he complains that the Egyptian troops have ill-treated his people, and that the officer who is with him has slandered him before the king ; he further declares that two of his towns have been taken from him, but that he will defend to the last whatever still remains of his patrimony.

Malchiel, the colleague of Labai in his attack upon Gezer, as afterwards upon Ebed-Tob of Jerusalem, does not appear to have been of Beduin origin.

But as long as the Beduin chief could be of use to him he was very willing to avail himself of his assistance, and it was always easy to drop the alliance as soon as it became embarrassing. Malchiel was the son-in-law of Tagi of Gath, and the colleague of Su-yardata, one of the few Canaanite governors whom the Egyptian government seems to have been able to trust. Both Su-yardata and Malchiel held commands in Southern Palestine, and we hear a good deal about them from Ebed-Tob. "The two sons of Malchiel" are also mentioned in a letter from a lady who bears a Babylonian name, and who refers to them in connection with an attempt to detach the cities of Ajalon and Zorah (Joshua xv. 33) from their allegiance to Egypt. The female correspondents of the Pharaoh are among the most curious and interesting features of the state of society depicted in the Tel el-Amarna tablets ; they entered keenly into the politics of the day, and kept the Egyptian king fully informed of all that was going on.

The letters of Ebed-Tob are so important that it is as well to give them in full. They all seem to have been written within a few months, or perhaps even weeks, of one another, when the enemies of the governor of Jerusalem were gathering around him, and no response came from Egypt to his requests for help. The dotted lines mark the words and passages which have been lost through the fracture of the clay tablets.

(I.) " To the king my lord [my] Sun-god, thus

[speaks] Ebed-Tob thy servant: at the feet of the king my lord seven times seven I prostrate myself. Behold, the king has established his name at the rising of the sun and the setting of the sun. Slanders have been uttered against me. Behold, I am not a governor, a vassal of the king my lord. Behold, I am an ally of the king, and I have paid the tribute due to the king, even I. Neither my father nor my mother, but the oracle (or arm) of the Mighty King established [me] in the house of [my] fathers. . . . There have come to me as a present 13 [women] and 10 slaves. Suta (Seti) the Commissioner of the king has come to me: 21 female slaves and 20 male slaves captured in war have been given into the hands of Suta as a gift for the king my lord, as the king has ordained for his country. The country of the king is being destroyed, all of it. Hostilities are carried on against me as far as the mountains of Seir (Joshua xv. 10) and the city of Gath-Karmel (Joshua xv. 55). All the other governors are at peace, but there is war against myself, since I see the foe, but I do not see the tears of the king my lord because war has been raised against me. While there is a ship in the midst of the sea, the arm (or oracle) of the Mighty King shall conquer the countries of Naharaim (Nakhrima) and Babylonia. But now the Confederates (Khabiri) are capturing the fortresses of the king. Not a single governor remains among them to the king my lord; all have perished. Behold, Turbazu, thy military officer, [has fallen] in

the great gate of the city of Zelah (Josh. xviii. 28).
Behold, Zimrida of Lachish has been murdered by
the servants who have revolted against the king.
Jephthah-Hadad, thy military officer, has been
slain in the great gate of Zelah. . . . May the king
[my lord] send help [to his country] ! May the
king turn his face to [his subjects] ! May he despatch troops to [his] country ! [Behold,] if no
troops come this year, all the countries of the king
my lord will be utterly destroyed. They do not
say before the face of the king my lord that the
country of the king my lord is destroyed, and that
all the governors are destroyed, if no troops come
this year. Let the king send a commissioner, and
let him come to me, even to me, with auxiliary
troops, and we will die with the king [our] lord.—
[To] the secretary of the king my lord [speaks]
Ebed-Tob [thy] servant. At [thy] feet [I prostrate
myself]. Let a report of [my] words be laid
before the king [my] lord. Thy [loyal] servant
am I."

(II.) " To the king my lord thus speaks Ebed-
Tob thy servant : at the feet of the king my lord
seven times seven I prostrate myself. What have
I done against the king my lord ? They have
slandered me, laying wait for me in the presence of
the king, the lord, saying : Ebed-Tob has revolted
from the king his lord. Behold, neither my father
nor my mother has exalted me in this place ; the
prophecy of the Mighty King has caused me to
enter the house of my father. Why should I have

committed a sin against the king the lord? With
the king my lord is life. I say to the officer of the
king [my] lord : Why dost thou love the Confederates and hate the governors? And constantly I
am sending to the presence of the king my lord to
say that the countries of the king my lord are
being destroyed. Constantly I am sending to the
king my lord, and let the king my lord consider,
since the king my lord has appointed the men of
the guard who have taken the fortresses. Let
Yikhbil-Khamu [be sent]. . . . . . . Let the king
send help to his country. [Let him send troops] to
his country which protects the fortresses of the
king my lord, all of them, since Elimelech is destroying all the country of the king ; and let the
king send help to his country. Behold, I have
gone down along with the king my lord, and I
have not seen the tears of the king my lord ; but
hostility is strong against me, yet I have not taken
anything whatever from the king my lord ; and let
the king incline towards my face ; let him despatch
a guard [for me], and let him appoint a commissioner, and I shall not see the tears of the king my
lord, since the king [my] lord shall live when the
commissioner has departed. Behold, the countries
of the king [my lord] are being destroyed, yet thou
dost not listen to me. All the governors are destroyed ; no governor remains to the king the lord.
Let the king turn his face to his subjects, and let
him send auxiliaries, even the troops of the king
my lord. No provinces remain unto the king ;

the confederates have wasted all the provinces of the king. If auxiliaries come this year, the provinces of the king the lord will be preserved ; but if no auxiliaries come the provinces of the king - my lord are destroyed.—[To] the secretary of the king my lord Ebed-Tob [says :] Give a report of my words to the king my lord : the provinces of the king my lord are being destroyed by the enemy."

(III.) "[To] the king my lord [speaks] Ebed-Tob [thy] servant : [at the feet of the king] my lord seven [times seven I prostrate myself. Behold, let] the king [listen to] the words [of his servant].
. . . . . . Let [the king] consider all the districts which are leagued in hostility against me, and let the king send help to his country. Behold, the country of the city of Gezer, the country of the city of Ashkelon and the city of La[chish] have given as their peace offerings food and oil and whatsoever the fortress needs. And let the king send help to his troops ; let him despatch troops against the men who have rebelled against the king my lord. If troops come this year, there will remain both provinces [and] governors to the king my lord ; [but] if no troops arrive, there will remain no provinces or governors to the king [my lord]. Behold, neither my father nor my mother has given this country of the city of Jerusalem unto me : it was an oracle [of the Mighty King] that gave it to me, even to me. Behold, Malchiel and the sons of Labai have given the country of the king to the

Confederates. Behold, the king my lord is righteous towards me. As to the Babylonians, let the
king ask the commissioner how very strong is the
temple-[fortress of Jerusalem.] . . . . . . Thou
hast delivered (?) the provinces into the hands of
the city of Ash[kelon]. Let the king demand of
them abundance of food, abundance of oil, and
abundance of wine until Pa-ur, the commissioner
of the king, comes up to the country of the city of
Jerusalem to deliver Adai along with the garrison
and the [rest of the people]. Let the king consider
the [instructions] of the king ; [let him] speak to
me ; let Adai deliver me—Thou wilt not desert it,
even this city, sending to me a garrison [and] sending a royal commissioner. Thy grace [is] to send
[them]. To the king [my lord] I have despatched
[a number of] prisoners [and a number of] slaves.
[I have looked after] the roads of the king in the
plain (*kikkar*, Gen. xiii. 10) and in the mountains.
Let the king my lord consider the city of Ajalon.
I am not able to direct my way to the king my
lord according to his instructions. Behold, the
king has established his name in the country of
Jerusalem for ever, and he cannot forsake the territories of the city of Jerusalem.—To the secretary
of the king my lord thus speaks Ebed-Tob thy
servant. At thy feet I prostrate myself. Thy
servant am I. Lay a report of my words before
the king my lord. The vassal of the king am I.
Mayest thou live long!—And thou hast performed
deeds which I cannot enumerate against the men

of the land of Ethiopia . . . The men of the country of the Babylonians [shall never enter] into my house . . . "

(IV.) (The beginning of the letter is lost, and it is not certain that Ebed-Tob was the writer of it.) "And now as to the city of Jerusalem, if this country is still the king's, why is Gaza made the seat of the king's government? Behold, the district of the city of Gath-Carmel has fallen away to Tagi and the men of Gath. He is in Bit-Sani (Beth-Sannah), and we have effected that they should give Labai and the country of the Sute to the men of the district of the Confederates. Malchiel has sent to Tagi and has seized some boy-slaves. He has granted all their requests to the men of Keilah, and we have delivered (or departed from) the city of Jerusalem. The garrison thou hast left in it is under the command of Apis the son of Miya-riya (Meri-Ra). Hadad-el has remained in his house in Gaza. . . ."

(V.) "To the king my lord thus [speaks] Ebed-Tob thy servant: at the feet of my lord [the king] seven times seven [I prostrate myself]. Behold, Malchiel does not separate himself from the sons of Labai and the sons of Arzai to demand the country of the king for themselves. As for the governor who acts thus, why does not the king question him? Behold, Malchiel and Tagi are they who have acted so, since they have taken the city of Rubute (Rabbah, Josh. xv. 60). . . . (Many lines are lost here.) There is no royal garrison [in Jerusalem]. May the king live eternally! Let Pa-ur go down to him. He has departed in front of me and is in the city of Gaza ; and let the king send to him a guard to defend the country. All the country of the king has revolted! Direct Yikhbil-Khamu [to come], and let him consider the country of the king [my lord].—To the secretary of the king [my lord] thus [speaks] Ebed-Tob thy servant : [at thy feet I prostrate myself]. Lay [a report] of my words [before] the king. Mayest thou live long! Thy servant am I."

(VI.) "[To] the king my lord thus speaks Ebed-Tob thy servant : at the feet of the king my lord seven times seven I prostrate myself. [The king knows the deed] which they have done, even Malchiel and Su-ardatum, against the country of the king my lord, commanding the forces of the city of Gezer, the forces of the city of Gath, and the forces of the city of Keilah. They have seized the district of the city of Rabbah. The country of the king has gone over to the Confederates. And now at this moment the city of the mountain of Jerusalem, the city of the temple of the god Nin-ip, whose name is Salim (?),[1] the city of the king, is gone over to the side of the men of Keilah. Let the king listen to Ebed-Tob thy servant, and let him despatch troops and restore the country of the king to the king. But if no troops arrive, the country of the king is gone over to the men

---

[1] Or, adopting the reading of Dr. Zimmern, " The city whose name is Bit-Nin-ip."

even to the Confederates. This is the deed [of Su-ar]datun and Malchiel. . . ."

The loyalty of Ebed-Tob, however, seems to have been doubted at the Egyptian court, where more confidence was placed in his rival and enemy Su-ardata (or Su-yardata, as the owner of the name himself writes it). Possibly the claim of the vassal-king of Jerusalem to have been appointed to his royal office by the " Mighty King " rather than by the "great king" of Egypt, and con- sequently to be an ally of the Pharaoh and not an ordinary governor, may have had something to do with the suspicions that were entertained of him. At all events we learn from a letter of Su-yardata that the occupation of Keilah by Ebed- Tob's enemies, of which the latter complains so bitterly, was due to the orders of the Egyptian government itself. Su-yardata there says—" The king [my lord] directed me to make war in the city of Keilah : war was made ; (and now) a complaint is brought against me. My city against myself has risen upon me. Ebed-Tob sends to the men of the city of Keilah ; he sends silver, and they have marched against my rear. And the king knows that Ebed-Tob has taken my city from my hand." The writer adds that "now Labai has taken Ebed-Tob and they have taken our cities." In his subsequent despatches to the home govern- ment Su-yardata complains that he is " alone," and asks that troops should be sent to him, saying that he is forwarding some *almehs* or maidens as a

K

present along with his "dragoman." At this point the correspondence breaks off.

Malchiel and Tagi also write to the Pharaoh. According to Tagi the roads between Southern Palestine and Egypt were under the supervision and protection of his brother; while Malchiel begs for cavalry to pursue and capture the enemy who had made war upon Su-yardata and himself, had seized "the country of the king," and threatened to slay his servants. He also complains of the conduct of Yankhamu, the High Commissioner, who had been ordered to inquire into the conduct of the governors in Palestine. Yankhamu, it seems, had seized Malchiel's property and carried off his wives and children. It was doubtless to this act of injustice that Labai alludes in his letter of exculpation.

The territory of which Jerusalem was the capital extended southward as far as Carmel of Judah, Gath-Carmel as it is called by Ebed-Tob, as well as in the geographical lists of Thothmes III., while on the west it reached to Keilah, Rabbah, and Mount Seir. No mention is made of Hebron either in the Tel el-Amarna letters or in the Egyptian geographical lists, which are earlier than the rise of the nineteenth dynasty. The town must therefore have existed under some other name, or have been in the hands of a power hostile to Egypt.

The name of Hebron has the same origin as that of the Khabiri, who appear in Ebed-Tob's letters by the side of Labai, Babylonia, and

Naharaim as the assailants of Jerusalem and its territory. The word means "Confederates," and occurs in the Assyrian texts ; among other passages in a hymn published by Dr. Brünnow, where we read, *istu pan khabiri-ya iptarsanni*, "from the face of my associates he has cut me off." The word, however, is not Assyrian, as in that case it would have had a different form, but must have been borrowed from the Canaanitish language of the West.

Who the Khabiri or "Confederates" were has been disputed. Some scholars see in them Elamite marauders who followed the march of the Babylonian armies to Syria. This opinion is founded on the fact that the Khabiri are once mentioned as an Elamite tribe, and that in a Babylonian document a "Khabirite" (*Khabirâ*) is referred to along with a "Kassite" or Babylonian. Another view is that they are to be identified with Heber, the grandson of Asher (Gen. xlvi. 17), since Malchiel is said to be the brother of Heber, just as in the letters of Ebed-Tob Malchiel is associated with the Khabiri. But all such identifications are based upon the supposition that "Khabiri" is a proper name rather than a descriptive title. Any band of "Confederates" could be called Khabiri whether in Elam or in Palestine, and it does not follow that the two bands were the same. In the "Confederates" of Southern Canaan we have to look for a body of confederated tribes who made themselves formidable to the governor of Jerusalem in the closing days of the Egyptian empire.

It would seem that Elimelech, who of course was a different person from Malchiel, was their leader, and as Elimelech is a Canaanitish name, we may conclude that the majority of his followers were also of Canaanitish descent. The scene of their hostilities was to the south of Jerusalem. Gath-Carmel, Zelah, and Lachish are the towns mentioned in connection with their attempts to capture and destroy "the fortresses of the king." "The country of the king" which had "gone over to the Confederates" was the territory over which Ebed-Tob claimed rule, while the district occupied by Labai and his Beduin followers was handed over "to the men of the district of the Confederates." The successes of the latter were gained through the intrigues of Malchiel and the sons of Labai.

All this leads us to the neighbourhood of Hebron, and suggests the question whether "the district of the Confederates" was not that of which Hebron, "the Confederacy," was the central meeting-place and sanctuary. Hebron has preserved its sacred character down to the present day; it long disputed with Jerusalem the claim of being the oldest and most hallowed shrine in Southern Palestine, and it was for many years the capital of Judah. Moreover, we know that "Hebron" was not the only name the city possessed. When Abram was "confederate" with the three Amorite chieftains it was known as Mamre (Gen. xiii. 18), and at a later day under the rule of the three sons of Anak it was called Kirjath-Arba.

According to the Biblical narrative Hebron was at once Amorite, Hittite, and Canaanite. Here, therefore, there was a confederation of tribes and races who would have met together at a common sanctuary. When Ezekiel says that Jerusalem was both Hittite and Amorite in its parentage, he may have been referring to its conquest and settlement by such a confederacy as that of Hebron. At all events we learn from Su-yardata's letter that Ebed-Tob eventually fell into the hands of his enemies; he was captured by Labai, and it is possible that his city became at the same time the prey of the Khabiri.

But all this is speculation, which may or may not prove to be correct. All we can be sure of is that the Khabiri or " Confederates " had their seat in the southern part of Palestine, and that we need not go outside Canaan to discover who they were. Ebed-Tob, at all events, carefully distinguishes them from either the Babylonians or the people of Naharaim.

In his letters, as everywhere else in the Tel el-Amarna correspondence, the Babylonians are called Kassi or Kassites. The name is written differently in the cuneiform texts from that of the Ethiopians, the Kash of the hieroglyphic inscriptions. Both, however, are alike represented in Hebrew by Cush, and hence we have not only a Cush who is the brother of Mizraim, but also another Cush who is the father of Nimrod. The name of the latter takes us back to the age of the Tel el-Amarna tablets.

Nahrima, or Naharaim, was the name by which
the kingdom of Mitanni was known to its Canaanite
and Egyptian neighbours. Mitanni, in fact, was
its capital, and it may be that Lutennu (or Lotan),
as the Egyptians called Syria and Palestine, was
but a mispronunciation of it. Along with the
Babylonians the people of Naharaim had made
themselves formidable to the inhabitants of Canaan,
and their name was feared as far south as Jerusalem. Even the governor of the Canaanite town
of Musikhuna, not far from the Sea of Galilee, bore
the Mitannian name of Sutarna. It was not,
indeed, until after the Israelitish conquest that the
last invasion of Canaan by a king of Aram-
Naharaim took place.

Gaza and Joppa were at one time under the
same governor, Yabitiri, who in a letter which has
come down to us asks to be relieved of the
burden of his office. Ashkelon, however, which
lay between the two sea-ports, was in the hands of
another prefect, Yidya by name, from whom we
have several letters, in one of which mention is
made of the Egyptian commissioner Rianap, or
Ra-nofer. The jurisdiction of Rianap extended
as far north as the plain of Megiddo, since he is
also referred to by Pu-Hadad, the governor of
Yurza, now Yerzeh, south-eastward of Taanach.
But it was more particularly in the extreme south
of Palestine that the duties of this officer lay.
Hadad-dan, who was entrusted with the government of Manahath and Tamar, to the west of the

Dead Sea, calls him "my Commissioner" in a letter in which he complains of the conduct of a certain Beya, the son of "the woman Gulat." Hadad-dan begins by saying that he had protected the commissioner and cities of the king, and then adds that "the city of Tumur is hostile to me, and I have built a house in the city of Mankhate, so that the household troops of the king my lord may be sent to me ; and lo, Bâya has taken it from my hand, and has placed his commissioner in it, and I have appealed to Rianap, my commissioner, and he has restored the city unto me, and has sent the household troops of the king my lord to me." After this the writer goes on to state that Beya had also intrigued against the city of Gezer, "the handmaid of the king my lord who created me." The rebel then carried off a quantity of plunder, and it became necessary to ransom his prisoners for a hundred pieces of silver, while those of his confederate were ransomed for thirty pieces of silver.

The misdeeds of Beya or Bâya did not end here. We hear of him again as attacking and capturing a body of soldiers who had been sent to defend the royal palace at Joppa, and as occupying that city itself. He was, however, subsequently expelled from it by the king's orders. Beya, too, professed to be an Egyptian governor and a faithful servant of the Pharaoh, to whom he despatched a letter to say that Yankhamu, the High Commissioner, was not in his district. Probably this was in answer to a charge brought against him by the Egyptian officer.

The official duties of Yankhamu extended over the whole of Palestine, and all the governors of its cities were accountable to him. We find him exercising his authority not only in the south, but also in the north, at Zemar and Gebal, and even among the Amorites. Amon-apt, to whom the superintendence of Phœnicia was more particularly entrusted, was supplied by him with corn, and frequent references are made to him in the letters of Rib-Hadad. Malchiel complained of his high-handed proceedings, and the complaint seems to have led to some confidential inquiries on the part of the home government, since we find a certain Sibti-Hadad writing in answer to the Pharaoh's questions that Yankhamu was a faithful servant of the king.

The country east of the Jordan also appears to have been within his jurisdiction. At all events the following letter was addressed to him by the governor Mut-Hadad, "the man of Hadad." "To Yankhamu my lord thus speaks Mut-Hadad thy servant: at the feet of my lord I prostrate myself. Since Mut-Hadad has declared in thy presence that Ayâb has fled, and it is certified (?) that the king of Bethel has fled from before the officers of the king his lord, may the king my lord live, may the king my lord live! I pray thee ask Ben-enima, ask . .tadua, ask Isuya, if Ayâb has been in this city of Bethel for [the last] two months. Ever

since the arrival of [the image of] the god Mero-
dach, the city of Astarti (Ashtaroth-Karnaim) has
been assisted, because all the fortresses of the
foreign land are hostile, namely, the cities of
Udumu (Edom), Aduri (Addar), Araru, Mestu
(Mosheh), Magdalim (Migdol), Khinianabi ('En
han-nabi), Zarki-tsabtat, Khaini ('En), and Ibi-
limma (Abel). Again after thou hadst sent a
letter to me I sent to him (*i. e.* Ayâb), [to wait]
until thy arrival from thy journey ; and he reached
the city of Bethel and [there] they heard the news."

We learn from this letter that Edom was a
"foreign country" unsubdued by the Egyptian
arms. The "city of Edom," from which the
country took its name, is again mentioned in the
inscriptions of the Assyrian king Esar-haddon,
and it was there that the Assyrian tax-gatherers
collected the tribute of the Edomite nation. It
would seem that the land of Edom stretched
further to the north in the age of Khu-n-Aten than
it did at a subsequent period of history, and that
it encroached upon what was afterwards the territory of Moab. The name of the latter country is
met with for the first time among the Asiatic
conquests of Ramses II. engraved on the base of
one of the colossal figures which stand in front of
the northern pylon of the temple of Luxor ; when
the Tel el-Amarna letters were written Moab was
included in the Canaanite province of Egypt.

A curious letter to Khu-n-Aten from Burna-
buryas, the Babylonian king, throws a good deal

of light on the nature of the Egyptian government in Canaan. Between the predecessors of the two monarchs there had been alliance and friendly intercourse, and nevertheless the Canaanitish subjects of the Pharaoh had committed an outrageous crime against some Babylonian merchants, which if left unpunished would have led to a rupture between the two countries. The merchants in question had entered Palestine under the escort of the Canaanite Ahitub, intending afterwards to visit Egypt. At Ên-athôn, near Acre, however, " in the country of Canaan," Sum-Adda, or Shem-Hadad, the son of Balumme (Balaam), and Sutatna, or Zid-athon, the son of Saratum,[1] who was governor of Acre, set upon them, killing some of them, maltreating others, and carrying away their goods. Burna-buryas therefore sent a special envoy, who was instructed to lay the following complaint before the Pharaoh : " Canaan is thy country and the king [of Acre is thy servant]. In thy country I have been injured ; do thou punish [the offenders]. The silver which they carried off was a present [for thee], and the men who are my servants they have slain. Slay them and requite the blood [of my servants]. But if thou dost not put these men to death, [the inhabitants] of the high-road that belongs to me will turn and verily will slay thy ambassadors, and a breach will be made in the agreement to respect the persons of ambassadors,

[1] His name is written Zurata in the letter of Biridî, the governor of Megiddo ; see above, p. 135.

and I shall be estranged from thee. Shem-Hadad, having cut off the feet of one of my men, has detained him with him ; and as for another man, Sutatna of Acre made him stand upon his head and then stood upon his face."

There are three letters in the Tel el-Amarna collection from Sutatna, or Zid-atna ("the god Zid has given ") as he writes his name, in one of which he compares Akku or Acre with "the city of Migdol in Egypt." Doubtless satisfaction was given to the Babylonian king for the wrong that had been done to his subjects, though whether the actual culprits were punished may be questioned. There is another letter from Burna-buryas, in which reference is again made to the Canaanites. He there asserts that in the time of his father, Kuri-galzu, they had sent to the Babylonian sovereign, saying : "Go down against Qannisat and let us rebel." Kuri-galzu, however, had refused to listen to them, telling them that if they wanted to break away from the Egyptian king and ally themselves "with another," they must find some one else to assist them. Burna-buryas goes on to declare that he was like-minded with his father, and had accordingly despatched an Assyrian vassal to assure the Pharaoh that he would carry on no intrigues with disaffected Canaanites. As the first part of his letter is filled with requests for gold for the adornment of a temple he was building at Babylon, such an assurance was very necessary. The despatches of Rib-Hadad and Ebed-Tob, however, go to show that in spite of his professions of friendship, the Babylonian monarch was ready to afford secret help to the insurgents in Palestine. The Babylonians were not likely to forget that they had once been masters of the country, or to regard the Egyptian empire in Asia with other than jealous eyes.

The Tel el-Amarna correspondence breaks off suddenly in the midst of a falling empire, with its governors in Canaan fighting and intriguing one against the other, and appealing to the Pharaoh for help that never came. The Egyptian commissioners are vainly endeavouring to restore peace and order, like General Gordon in the Soudan, while Babylonians and Mitannians, Hittites and Beduin are assailing the distracted province. The Asiatic empire of the eighteenth dynasty, however, did not wholly perish with the death of Khu-n-Aten. A picture in the tomb of prince Hui at Thebes shows that under the reign of his successor, Tut-ankh-Amon, the Egyptian supremacy was still acknowledged in some parts of Syria. The chiefs of the Lotan or Syrians are represented in their robes of many colours, some with white and others with brown skins, and coming before the Egyptian monarch with the rich tribute of their country. Golden trays full of precious stones, vases of gold and silver, the covers of which are in the form of the heads of gazelles and other animals, golden rings richly enamelled, horses, lions, and a leopard's skin—such are the gifts which they offer to the

Pharaoh. It was the last embassy of the kind which was destined to come from Syria for many a day.

With the rise of the nineteenth dynasty and the restoration of a strong government at home, the Egyptians once more began to turn their eyes towards Palestine. Seti I. drove the Beduin before him from the frontiers of Egypt to those of "Canaan," and established a line of fortresses and wells along "the way of the Philistines," which ran by the shore of the Mediterranean to Gaza. The road was now open for him to the north along the sea-coast. We hear accordingly of his capture of Acre, Tyre, and Usu or Palætyros, from whence he marched into the Lebanon and took Kumidi and Inu'am. One of his campaigns must have led him into the interior of Palestine, since in his list of conquered cities we find the names of Carmel and Beth-anoth, of Beth-el and Pahil or Pella, as well as of Qamham or Chimham (see Jer. xli. 17). Kadesh, "in the land of the Amorites," was captured by a sudden assault, and Seti claims to have defeated or received the submission of Alasiya and Naharaim, the Hittites and the Assyrians, Cyprus and Sangar. It would seem, however, that north of Kadesh he really made his way only along the coast as far as the Gulf of Antioch and Cilicia, overrunning towns and districts of which we know little more than the names.

Seti was succeeded by his son Ramses II., the

Pharaoh of the Oppression, and the builder of Pithom and Ramses. His long reign of sixty-seven years lasted from 1348 B.C. to 1281 B.C. The first twenty-one years of it were occupied in the re-conquest of Palestine, and sanguinary wars with the Hittites. But these mountaineers of the north had established themselves too firmly in the old Egyptian province of Northern Syria to be dislodged. All the Pharaoh could effect was to stop their further progress towards the south, and to save Canaan from their grasp. The war between the two great powers of Western Asia ended at last through the sheer exhaustion of the rival combatants. A treaty of alliance, offensive and defensive, was drawn up between Ramses II. and Khata-sil, "the great king of the Hittites," and it was cemented by the marriage of the Pharaoh to the daughter of the Hittite prince. Syria was divided between the Hittites and Egyptians, and it was agreed that neither should under any pretext invade the territories of the other. It was also agreed that if either country was attacked by foreign foes or rebellious subjects, the other should come to its help. Political refugees, moreover, were to be delivered up to the sovereign from whom they had escaped, but it was stipulated that in this case they should receive a full pardon for the offences they had committed. The Hittite copy of the treaty was engraved on a silver plate, and the gods of Egypt and the Hittites were called upon to witness the execution of it.

The legendary exploits of Sesostris, that creation of Greek fancy and ignorance, were fastened upon Ramses II., whose long reign, inordinate vanity, and ceaseless activity as a builder made him one of the most prominent of the old Pharaohs. It was natural, therefore, at the beginning of hieroglyphic decipherment that the Greek accounts should be accepted in full, and that Ramses II. should have been regarded as the greatest of Egyptian conquerors. But further study soon showed that, in this respect at least, his reputation had little to support it. Like his monuments, too, many of which are really stolen from his predecessors, or else sacrifice honesty of work to haste and pretentiousness, a large part of the conquests and victories that have been claimed for him was due to the imagination of the scribes. In the reaction which followed on this discovery, the modern historians of ancient Egypt were disposed to dispute his claim to be a conqueror at all. But we now know that such a scepticism was exaggerated, and though Ramses II. was not a conqueror like Thothmes III., he nevertheless maintained and extended the Asiatic empire which his father had recovered, and the lists of vanquished cities which he engraved on the walls of his temples were not mere repetitions of older catalogues, or the empty fictions of flattering chroniclers. Egyptian armies really marched once more into Northern Syria and the confines of Cilicia, and probably made their way to the banks of the Euphrates. We have no reason for denying that Assyrian troops may have been defeated by his arms, or that the king of Mitanni may have sent an embassy to his court. And we now have a good deal more than the indirect evidence of the treaty with the Hittites to show that Canaan was again a province of the Egyptian empire. The names of some of its cities which were captured in the early part of the Pharaoh's reign may still be read on the walls of the Ramesseum at Thebes. Among them are Ashkelon, Shalam or Jerusalem, Merom, and Beth-Anath, which were taken by storm in his eighth year. Dapul, "in the land of the Amorites," was captured at the same time, proving that the Egyptian forces penetrated as far as the Hittite frontiers. At Luxor other Canaanite names figure in the catalogue of vanquished states. Thus we have Carmel of Judah, Ir-shemesh and Hadashah (Josh. xv. 37), Gaza, Sela and Jacob-el, Socho, Yurza, and Korkha in Moab. The name of Moab itself appears for the first time among the subject nations, while we gather from a list of mining settlements, that Cyprus as well as the Sinaitic peninsula was under Egyptian authority.

A sarcastic account of the misadventures of a military officer in Palestine, which was written in the time of Ramses, is an evidence of the complete occupation of that country by the Egyptians. All parts of Canaan are alluded to in it, and as Dr. Max Müller has lately pointed out, we find in it for the first time the names of Shechem and

Kirjath-Sepher. Similar testimony is borne by a hieroglyphic inscription recently discovered by Dr. Schumacher on the so-called "Stone of Job" in the Haurân. The stone (*Sakhrat 'Ayyub*) is a monolith westward of the Sea of Galilee, and not far from Tel 'Ashtereh, the ancient Ashtaroth-Karnaim, which was a seat of Egyptian government in the time of Khu-n-Aten. The monolith is adorned with Egyptian sculptures and hieroglyphs. One of the sculptures represents a Pharaoh above whose likeness is the cartouche of Ramses II., while opposite the king, to the left, is the figure of a god who wears the crown of Osiris, but has a full face. Over the god is his name in hieroglyphics. The name, however, is not Egyptian, but seems to be intended for the Canaanite Yakin-Zephon or "Yakin of the North." It is plain, therefore, that we have here a monument testifying to the rule of Ramses II., but a monument which was erected by natives of the country to a native divinity. For a while the hieroglyphic writing of Egypt had taken the place formerly occupied by the cuneiform syllabary of Babylonia, and Egyptian culture had succeeded in supplanting that which had come from the East.

The nineteenth dynasty ended even more disastrously than the eighteenth. It is true that the great confederacy of northern and Libyan tribes which attacked Egypt by sea and land in the reign of Meneptah, the son and successor of Ramses II., was successfully repulsed, but the

L

energy of the Egyptian power seemed to exhaust itself in the effort. The throne fell into the hands of usurpers, and the house of Ramses was swept away by civil war and anarchy. The government was seized by a Syrian, Arisu by name, and for a time Egypt was compelled to submit to a foreign yoke. The overthrow of the foreigner and the restoration of the native monarchy was due to the valour of Set-nekht, the founder of the twentieth dynasty and the father of Ramses III.

It was under one of the immediate successors of Ramses II. that the exodus of the Israelites out of Egypt must have taken place. Egyptian tradition pointed to Meneptah ; modern scholars incline rather to his successors Seti II. and Si-Ptah. With this event the patriarchal history of Canaan ought properly to come to an end. But the Egyptian monuments still cast light upon it, and enable us to carry it on almost to the moment when Joshua and his followers entered the Promised Land.

Palestine still formed part of the kingdom of Meneptah, at all events in the earlier years of his reign. A scribe has left us a record of the officials who passed to and from Canaan through the frontier fortress of Zaru during the middle of the month Pakhons in the third year of the king. One of these was Baal–. . . the son of Zippor of Gaza, who carried a letter for the Egyptian overseer of the Syrian peasantry (or Perizzites), as well as another for Baal-[sa]lil-ga[b]u, the vassal-prince of Tyre.

Another messenger was Sutekh-mes, the son of 'Aper-dagar, who also carried a despatch to the overseer of the peasantry, while a third envoy came in the reverse direction, from the city of Meneptah, "in the land of the Amorites."

In the troubles which preceded the accession of the twentieth dynasty the Asiatic possessions of Egypt were naturally lost, and were never again recovered. Ramses III., however, the last of the conquering Pharaohs, made at least one campaign in Palestine and Syria. Like Meneptah, he had to bear the brunt of an attack upon Egypt by the confederated hordes of the north which threatened to extinguish its civilization altogether. The nations of Asia Minor and the Ægean Sea had poured into Syria as the northern barbarians in later days poured into the provinces of the Roman Empire. Partly by land, partly by sea, they made their way through Phœnicia and the land of the Hittites, destroying everything as they went, and carrying in their train the subjugated princes of Naharaim and Kadesh. For a time they encamped in the "land of the Amorites," and then pursued their southward march. Ramses III. met them on the north-eastern frontier of his kingdom, and in a fiercely-contested battle utterly overthrew them. The ships of the invaders were captured or sunk, and their forces on land were decimated. Immense quantities of booty and prisoners were taken, and the shattered forces of the enemy retreated into Syria. There the Philistines and Zakkal possessed themselves of the sea-coast, and garrisoned the cities of the extreme south. Gaza ceased to be an Egyptian fortress, and became instead an effectual barrier to the Egyptian occupation of Canaan.

When Ramses III. followed the retreating invaders of his country into Syria, it is doubtful whether the Philistines had as yet settled themselves in their future home. At all events Gaza fell into his hands, and he found no difficulty in marching along the Mediterranean coast like the conquering Pharaohs who had preceded him. In his temple palace at Medînet Habu he has left a record of the conquests that he made in Syria. The great cities of the coast were untouched. No attempt was made to besiege or capture Tyre and Sidon, Beyrout and Gebal, and the Egyptian army marched past them, encamping on the way only at such places as "the headland of Carmel," "the source of the Magoras," or river of Beyrout, and the Bor or "Cistern." Otherwise its resting-places were at unknown villages like Inzath and Lui-el. North of Beyrout it struck eastward through the gorge of the Nahr el-Kelb, and took the city of Kumidi. Then it made its way by Shenir or Hermon to Hamath, which surrendered, and from thence still northward to "the plain" of Aleppo.

In the south of Palestine, in what was afterwards the territory of Judah, Ramses made yet another campaign. Here he claims to have taken Lebanoth and Beth-Anath, Carmel of Judah and Shebtîn, Jacob-el and Hebron, Libnah and Aphek,

Migdal-gad and Ir-Shemesh, Hadashah and the district of Salem or Jerusalem.   From thence the Egyptian forces proceeded to the Lake of Reshpon or the Dead Sea, and then crossing the Jordan seized Korkha in Moab.   But the campaign was little more than a raid ; it left no permanent results behind it, and all traces of Egyptian authority disappeared with the departure of the Pharaoh's army.   Canaan remained the prey of the first resolute invader who had strength and courage at his back.

CHAPTER IV

THE PATRIARCHS

ABRAHAM had been born in " Ur of the Chaldees." Ur lay on the western side of the Euphrates in Southern Babylonia, where the mounds of Muqayyar or Mugheir mark the site of the great temple that had been reared to the worship of the Moon-god long before the days of the Hebrew patriarch. Here Abraham had married, and from hence he had gone forth with his father to seek a new home in the west. Their first resting-place had been Harran in Mesopotamia, on the high-road to Syria and the Mediterranean. The name of Harran, in fact, signified "road" in the old language of Chaldæa, and for many ages the armies and merchants of Babylonia had halted there when making their way towards the Mediterranean. Like Ur, it was dedicated to the worship of Sin, the Moon-god, and its temple rivalled in fame and antiquity that of the Babylonian city, and had probably been founded by a Babylonian king.

At Harran, therefore, Abraham would still have been within the limits of Babylonian influence and culture, if not of Babylonian government as well. He would have found there the same religion as that which he had left behind him in his native city ; the same deity was adored there, under the same name and with the same rites. He was indeed on the road to Canaan, and among an Aramæan rather than a Babylonian population, but Babylonia with its beliefs and civilization had not as yet been forsaken. Even the language of Babylonia was known in his new home, as is indicated by the name of the city itself.

Harran and Mesopotamia were not the goal of the future father of the Israelitish people. He was bidden to seek elsewhere another country and another kindred. Canaan was the land which God promised to "show" to him, and it was in Canaan that his descendants were to become "a great nation." He went forth, accordingly, "to go into the land of Canaan, and into the land of Canaan he came."

But even in Canaan Abraham was not beyond the reach of Babylonian influence. As we have seen in the last chapter, Babylonian armies had already penetrated to the shores of the Mediterranean, Palestine had been included within the bounds of a Babylonian empire, and Babylonian culture and religion had spread widely among the Canaanitish tribes. The cuneiform system of writing had made its way to Syria, and Babylonian literature had followed in its wake. Centuries had already passed since Sargon of Akkad had made himself master of the Mediterranean coast and his son Naram-Sin had led his forces to the Peninsula of Sinai. Istar of Babylonia had become Ashtoreth of the Canaanites, and Babylonian trade had long moved briskly along the very road that Abraham traversed. In the days of the patriarch himself the rulers of Babylonia claimed to be also rulers of Canaan; for thirteen years did the Canaanite princes "serve" Chedor-laomer and his allies, the father of Arioch is also "the father of the land of the Amorites" in his son's inscriptions, and at a little later date the King of Babylon still claimed sovereignty over the West.

It was not, therefore, to a strange and unexplored country that Abraham had migrated. The laws and manners to which he had been accustomed, the writing and literature which he had learned in the schools of Ur, the religious beliefs among which he had lived in Chaldæa and Harran, he found again in Canaan. The land of his adoption was full of Babylonian traders, soldiers, and probably officials as well, and from time to time he must have heard around him the language of his birth-place. The introduction into the West of the Babylonian literature and script brought with it a knowledge of the Babylonian language, and the knowledge is reflected in some of the local names of Palestine. The patriarch had not escaped beyond the control even of the Babylonian government. At times, at all events, the princes of Canaan were compelled to acknowledge the suzerainty of Chaldæa and obey the laws, as the Babylonians would have said, of " Anu and Dagon."

The fact needs dwelling upon, partly because of its importance, partly because it is but recently that we have begun to realize it. It might indeed have been gathered from the narratives of Genesis, more especially from the account of Chedor-laomer's campaign, but it ran counter to the preconceived ideas of the modern historian, and never therefore took definite shape in his mind. It is one of the many gains that the decipherment of the cuneiform inscriptions has brought to the student of the Old Testament, and it makes us understand the story of Abraham's migration in a way that was never possible before. He was no wild nomad wandering in unknown regions, among a people of alien habits and foreign civilization. We know now why he took the road which we are told he followed ; why he was able to make allies among the inhabitants of Canaan ; why he understood their language and could take part in their social life. Like the Englishman who migrates to a British colony, Abraham was in contact with the same culture in Canaan and Chaldæa alike.

But when he reached Canaan he was not yet Abraham. He was still " Abram the Hebrew," and it was as " Abram the Hebrew " that he made alliance with the Amorites of Mamre and overthrew the retreating forces of the Babylonian kings. Abram—Abu-ramu, " the exalted father,"—is a Babylonian name, and is found in contracts of the age of Chedor-laomer. When the name was changed to Abraham, it was a sign that the Babylonian emigrant had become a native of the West.

It was under the terebinth of Moreh before Shechem that Abraham first pitched his tent and erected his first altar to the Lord. Above him towered Ebal and Gerizim, where the curses and blessings of the Law were afterwards to be pronounced. From thence he moved southward to one of the hills westward of Beth-el, the modern Beitin, and there his second altar was built. While the first had been reared in the plain, the second was raised on the mountain-slope.

But here too he did not remain long. Again he " journeyed, going on still towards the south." Then came a famine which obliged him to cross the frontier of Egypt, and visit the court of the Pharaoh. The Hyksos kinsmen of the race to which he belonged were ruling in the Delta, and a ready welcome was given to the Asiatic stranger. He was " very rich in cattle, in silver and in gold," and like a wealthy Arab sheikh to-day was received with due honour in the Egyptian capital. The court of the Pharaoh was doubtless at Zoan.

Among the possessions of the patriarch we are told were camels. The camel is not included among the Egyptian hieroglyphs, nor has it been found depicted on the walls of the Egyptian temples and tombs. The name is first met with in a papyrus of the time of the nineteenth dynasty, and is one of the many words which the Egyptians of that age borrowed from their Canaanitish neigh-bours. The animal, in fact, was not used by the Egyptians, and its domestication in the valley of the Nile seems to be as recent as the Arab conquest. But though it was not used by the Egyptians, it had been a beast of burden among the Semites of Arabia from an early period. In the primitive Sumerian language of Chaldæa it was called "the animal from the Persian Gulf," and its Semitic name, from which our own word *camel* is derived, goes back to the very beginnings of Semitic history. We cannot, therefore, imagine a Semitic nomad arriving in Egypt without the camel ; travellers, indeed, from the cities of Canaan might do so, but not those who led a purely nomadic life. And, in fact, though we look in vain for a picture of the camel among the sculptures and paintings of Egypt, the bones of the animal have been discovered deep in the alluvial soil of the valley of the Nile.

Abraham had to quit Egypt, and once more he traversed the desert of the "South" and pitched his tent near Beth-el. Here his nephew Lot left him, and, dissatisfied with the life of a wandering Bedawi, took up his abode in the city of Sodom at the northern end of the Dead Sea. While Abraham kept himself separate from the natives of Canaan, Lot thus became one of them, and narrowly escaped the doom which afterwards fell upon the cities of the plain. In forsaking the tent, he forsook not only the free life of the immigrant from Chaldæa, but the God of Abraham as well. The inhabitant

of a Canaanitish city passed under the influence of
its faith and worship, its morals and manners, as
well as its laws and government. He ceased to be
an alien and stranger, of a different race and father-
land, and with a religion and customs of his own.
He could intermarry with the natives of his adopted
country and participate in their sacred rites. Little
by little his family became merged in the population
that surrounded him ; its gods became their gods,
its morality—or, it may be, its immorality—became
theirs also. Lot, indeed, had eventually to fly
from Sodom, leaving behind him all his wealth ;
but the mischief had already been done, and his
children had become Canaanites in thought and
deed. The nations which sprang from him, though
separate in race from the older people of Canaan,
were yet like them in other respects. They formed
no " peculiar people," to whom the Lord might
reveal Himself through the law and the prophets.

It was not until Lot had separated himself from
Abraham that the land of Canaan was promised to
the descendants of the patriarch. " Lift up now
thine eyes," God said to him, " and look from the
place where thou art, northward and southward,
and eastward and westward : for all the land which
thou seest, to thee will I give it, and to thy seed for
ever." Once more, therefore, Abraham departed
southward from Shechem ; not this time to go into
the land of Egypt, but to dwell beside the terebinth-
oak of Mamre hard by Hebron, where the founder
of the Davidic monarchy was hereafter to be

crowned king. It is probable that the sanctuary which in days to come was to make Hebron famous had not as yet been established there ; at all events the name of Hebron, " the confederacy," was not as yet known, and the city was called Kirjath-Arba. Whether it was also called Mamre is doubtful ; Mamre would rather seem to have been the name of the plateau which stretched beyond the valley of Hebron and was occupied by the Amorite confederates of the Hebrew patriarch.

It was while he "dwelt under the terebinth of Mamre the Amorite " that the campaign of Chedor-laomer and his Babylonian allies took place, and that Lot was carried away among the Canaanitish captives. But the triumph of the conquerors was short-lived. " Abram the Hebrew " pursued them with his armed followers, three hundred and eighteen in number, as well as with his Amorite allies, and suddenly falling upon their rear-guard near Damascus by night, rescued the captives and the spoil. There was rejoicing in the Canaanitish cities when the patriarch returned with his booty. The new king of Sodom met him in the valley of Shaveh, " the king's dale " of later times, just outside the walls of Jerusalem, and the king of Jerusalem himself, Melchizedek, " the priest of the most High God," welcomed the return of the victor with bread and wine. Then it was that Abram gave tithes of the spoil to the God of Salem, while Melchizedek blessed him in the name of " the most High God."

Outside the pages of the Old Testament the special form assumed by the blessing has been found only in the Aramaic inscriptions of Egypt. Here too we find travellers from Palestine writing of themselves " Blessed be Augah of Isis," or "Blessed be Abed-Nebo of Khnum"! It would seem, therefore, to have been a formula peculiar to Canaan; at all events, it has not been traced to other parts of the Semitic world. The temple of the Most High God—El Elyôn—probably stood on Mount Moriah where the temple of the God of Israel was afterwards to be erected. It will be remembered that among the letters sent by Ebed-Tob, the king of Jerusalem, to the Egyptian Pharaoh is one in which he speaks of "the city of the Mountain of Jerusalem, whose name is the city of the temple of the god Nin-ip." In this " Mountain of Jerusalem " it is difficult not to see the " temple-Mount " of later days.

In the cuneiform texts of Ebed-Tob and the later Assyrian kings the name of Jerusalem is written Uru-Salim, " the city of Salim." Salim or " Peace " is almost certainly the native name of the god who was identified with the Babylonian Nin-ip, and perhaps Isaiah—that student of the older history of his country—is alluding to the fact when he declares that one of the titles of the Messiah shall be "the Prince of Peace." At any rate, if the Most High God of Jerusalem were really Salim, the God of Peace, we should have an explanation of the blessing pronounced by Melchizedek upon the patriarch. Abram's victory had restored peace to Canaan ; he had brought back the captives, and had himself returned in peace. It was fitting, therefore, that he should be welcomed by the priest of the God of Peace, and that he should offer tithes of the booty he had recovered to the god of " the City of Peace."

This offering of tithes was no new thing. In his Babylonian home Abraham must have been familiar with the practice. The cuneiform inscriptions of Babylonia contain frequent references to it. It went back to the pre-Semitic age of Chaldæa, and the great temples of Babylonia were largely supported by the *esrâ* or tithe which was levied upon prince and peasant alike. That the god should receive a tenth of the good things which, it was believed, he had bestowed upon mankind, was not considered to be asking too much. There are many tablets in the British Museum which are receipts for the payment of the tithe to the great temple of the Sun-god at Sippara in the time of Nebuchadrezzar and his successors. From one of them we learn that Belshazzar, even at the very moment when the Babylonian empire was falling from his father's hands, nevertheless found an opportunity for paying the tithe due from his sister ; while others show us that Cyrus and Cambyses did not regard their foreign origin as affording any pretext for refusing to pay tithe to the gods of the kingdom they had overthrown.

The Babylonian army had been defeated near

Damascus, and immediately after this we are told
that the steward of Abraham's house was " Eli-ezer
of Damascus." Whether there is any connection
between the two facts we cannot say ; but it may
be that Eli-ezer had attached himself to the
Hebrew conqueror when he was returning " from
the slaughter of Chedor-laomer." The name of
Eli-ezer, " God is a help," is characteristic of
Damascus. More often in place of El, " God," we
have Hadad, the supreme deity of Syria ; but just as
among the Israelites Eli-akim and Jeho-iakim are
equivalent, so among the Aramæans of Syria were
Eli-ezer and Hadad-ezer. Hadad-ezer, it will be
remembered, was the king of Zobah who was overthrown by David.

Sarai, the wife of Abraham, was still childless,
but the patriarch had a son by his Egyptian handmaid, the ancestor of the Ishmaelite tribes who
spread from the frontier of Egypt to Mecca in
Central Arabia. It was when Ishmael was thirteen
years of age that the covenant was made between
God and Abraham which was sealed with the
institution of circumcision. Circumcision had been
practised in Egypt from the earliest days of its
history ; henceforth it also distinguished all those
who claimed Abraham as their forefather. With
circumcision Abraham received the name by which
he was henceforth to be known ; he ceased to be
Abram, the Hebrew from Babylonia, and became
Abraham the father of Ishmael and Israel. The
new rite and the new name were alike the seal and

token of the covenant established between the patriarch and his God : God promised that his seed should multiply, and that the land of Canaan should be given as an everlasting possession, while Abraham and his offspring were called upon to keep God's covenant for ever.

It could not have been long after this that the cities of the plain were destroyed " with brimstone and fire from the Lord out of heaven." The expression is found in the cuneiform tablets of Babylonia. Old Sumerian hymns spoke of a " rain of stones and fire," though the stones may have been hail-stones and thunderbolts, and the fire the flash of the lightning. But whatever may have been the nature of the sheet of flame which enveloped the guilty cities of the plain and set on fire the naphtha-springs that oozed out of it, the remembrance of the catastrophe survived to distant ages. The prophets of Israel and Judah still refer to the overthrow of Sodom and its sister cities, and St. Jude points to them as " suffering the vengeance of eternal fire." Some scholars have seen an allusion to their overthrow in the tradition of the Phœnicians which brought their ancestors into the coastlands of Canaan in consequence of an earthquake on the shores of " the Assyrian Lake." But the lake is more probably to be looked for in the neighbourhood of the Persian Gulf than in the valley of the Jordan.

The vale of Siddim, and " the cities of the plain," stood at the northern end of the Dead Sea. Here

M

were the "slime-pits" from which the naphtha was extracted, and which caused the defeat of the Canaanitish princes by the Babylonian army. The legend which placed the pillar of salt into which Lot's wife was changed at the southern extremity of the Dead Sea was of late origin, probably not earlier than the days when Herod built his fortress of Machærus on the impregnable cliffs of Moab, and the name of Gebel Usdum, given by the modern Arabs to one of the mountain-summits to the south of the sea proves nothing as to the site of the city of Sodom. Names in the east are readily transferred from one locality to another, and a mountain is not the same as a city in a plain.

There are two sufficient reasons why it is to the north rather than to the south that we must look for the remains of the doomed cities, among the numerous tumuli which rise above the rich and fertile plain in the neighbourhood of Jericho, where the ancient "slime - pits" can still be traced. Geology has taught us that throughout the historical period the Dead Sea and the country immediately to the south of it have undergone no change. What the lake is to-day, it must have been in the days of Abraham. It has neither grown nor shrunk in size, and the barren salt with which it poisons the ground must have equally poisoned it then. No fertile valley, like the vale of Siddim, could have existed in the south ; no prosperous Canaanitish cities could have grown up among the desolate tracts of the southern wilderness. As we are expressly told in the Book of Numbers (xiii. 29), the Canaanites dwelt only "by the coast of Jordan," not in the desert far beyond the reach of the fertilizing stream.

But there is another reason which excludes the southern site. "When Abraham got up early in the morning," we are told, "he looked towards Sodom and Gomorrah, and toward all the land of the plain, and beheld, and, lo, the smoke of the country went up as the smoke of a furnace." Such a sight was possible from the hills of Hebron, if the country lay at the northern end of the Dead Sea, it would have been impossible had it been south of it.

Moreover, the northern situation of the cities alone agrees with the geography of Genesis. When the Babylonian invaders had turned northwards after smiting the Amalekites of the desert south of the Dead Sea, they did not fall in with the forces of the king of Sodom and his allies until they had first passed "the Amorites that dwelt in Hazezon-tamar." Hazezon-tamar, as we learn from the Second Book of Chronicles (xx. 2), was the later En-gedi, "the Spring of the Kid," and En-gedi lay on the western shore of the Dead Sea midway between its northern and southern extremities.

In the warm, soft valley of the Jordan, accordingly, where a sub-tropical vegetation springs luxuriantly out of the fertile ground and the river plunges into the Dead Sea as into a tomb, the nations of Ammon and Moab were born. It was a fitting spot, in close proximity as it was to the countries which thereafter bore their names. From the mountain above Zoar, Lot could look across to the blue hills of Moab and the distant plateau of Ammon.

Meanwhile Abraham had quitted Mamre and again turned his steps towards the south. This time it was at Gerar, between the sanctuary of Kadesh-barnea and Shur the "wall" of Egypt that he sojourned. Kadesh has been found again in our own days by the united efforts of Dr. John Rowlands and Dr. Clay Trumbull in the shelter of a block of mountains which rise to the south of the desert of Beer-sheba. The spring of clear and abundant water which gushes forth in their midst was the En-Mishpat—" the spring where judgments were pronounced"—of early times, and is still called 'Ain-Qadîs, "the spring of Kadesh." Gerar is the modern Umm el-Jerâr, now desolate and barren, all that remains of its past being a lofty mound of rubbish and a mass of potsherds. It lies a few hours only to the south of Gaza.

Here Isaac was born and circumcised, and here Ishmael and Hagar were cast forth into the wilderness and went to dwell in the desert of Paran. The territory of Gerar extended to Beer-sheba, " the well of the oath," where Abraham's servants digged a well, and Abimelech, king of Gerar, confirmed his possession of it by an oath. It may be that one of the two wells which still exist at Wadi es-Seba', with the stones that line their mouths deeply indented by the ropes of the water-drawers, is the very one around which the herdsmen of Abraham and Abimelech wrangled with each other. The wells of the desert go back to a great antiquity : where water is scarce its discovery is not easily forgotten, and the Beduin come with their flocks year after year to drink of it. The old wells are constantly renewed, or new ones dug by their side.

Gerar was in that south-western corner of Palestine which in the age of the Exodus was inhabited by the Philistines. But they had been new-comers. All through the period of the eighteenth and nineteenth Egyptian dynasties the country had been in the hands of the Egyptians. Gaza had been their frontier fortress, and as late as the reign of Meneptah, the son of the Pharaoh of the Oppression, it was still garrisoned by Egyptian troops and governed by Egyptian officers. The Pulsata or Philistines did not arrive till the troublous days of Ramses III., of the twentieth dynasty. They formed part of the barbarian hordes from the shores of Asia Minor and the islands of the Ægean, who swarmed over Syria and flung themselves on the valley of the Nile, and the land of Caphtor from which they came was possibly the island of Krete. The Philistine occupation of the coast-land of Canaan, therefore, did not long precede the Israelitish invasion of the Promised Land ; indeed we may perhaps gather from the words of Exod. xiii. 17 that the Philistines were already winning for themselves their new territory when the Israelites marched out of Egypt. In saying, consequently, that the kingdom of Abimelech was in the land of the Philistines the Book of Genesis speaks proleptically : when the story of Abraham and Abimelech was written in its present form Gerar was a Philistine town : in the days of the patriarchs this was not yet the case.

At Beer-sheba Abraham planted a tamarisk, and "called on the name of the Lord, the everlasting God." Beer-sheba long remained one of the sacred places of Palestine. The tree planted by its well was a sign both of the water that flowed beneath its soil and of its sacred character. It was only where fresh water was found that the nomads of the desert could come together, and the tree was a token of the life and refreshment they would meet with. The well was sacred ; so also was the solitary tree which stood beside it, and under whose branches man and beast could find shade and protection from the mid-day heat. Even Mohammedanism, that Puritanism of the East, has not been able to eradicate the belief in the divine nature of such trees from the mind of the nomad ; we may still see them decorated with offerings of rags torn from the garments of the passer-by or shading the tomb of some reputed saint. They are still more than waymarks or resting-places for the heated and weary ; when standing beneath them the herdsman feels that he is walking upon consecrated ground.

It was at Beer-sheba that the temptation came
to Abraham to sacrifice his first-born, his only son
Isaac. The temptation was in accordance with
the fierce ritual of Syria, and traces of the belief
which had called it into existence are to be found
in the early literature of Babylonia. Thus in an
ancient Babylonian ritual-text we read : " The offspring who raises his head among mankind, the
offspring for his life he gave ; the head of the
offspring for the head of the man he gave ; the
neck of the offspring for the neck of the man he
gave." Phœnician legend told how the god El
had robed himself in royal purple and sacrificed
his only son Yeud in a time of pestilence, and the
writers of Greece and Rome describe with horror
the sacrifices of the first-born with which the
history of Carthage was stained. The father was
called upon in time of trouble to yield up to the
god his nearest and dearest ; the fruit of his body
could alone wipe away the sin of his soul, and Baal
required him to sacrifice without a murmur or a
tear his first-born and his only one. The more
precious the offering, the more acceptable was it
to the god ; the harder the struggle to resign it,
the greater was the merit of doing so. The child
died for the sins of his people ; and the belief was
but the blind and ignorant expression of a true
instinct.

But Abraham was to be taught a better way.
For three days he journeyed northward with his
son, and then lifting up his eyes saw afar off that

mountain "in the land of Moriah," on the summit of which the sacrifice was to be consummated. Alone with Isaac he ascended to the high-place, and there building his altar and binding to it his son he prepared to perform the terrible rite. But at the last moment his hand was stayed, a new and better revelation was made to him, and a ram was substituted for his son. It cannot be accidental that, as M. Clermont-Ganneau has pointed out, we learn from the temple-tariffs of Carthage and Marseilles that in the later ritual of Phœnicia a ram took the place of the earlier human sacrifice.

Where was this mountain in the land of Moriah whereon the altar of Abraham was built? It would seem from a passage in the Second Book of Chronicles (iii. 1) that it was the future temple-mount at Jerusalem. The words of Genesis also point in the same direction. Abraham, we read, "called the name of that place Jehovah-jireh : as it is said to this day, In the mount of the Lord it shall be seen." It is hard to believe that "the mount of the Lord" can mean anything else than that *har-el* or "mountain of God" whereon Ezekiel places the temple, or that the proverb can refer to a less holy spot than that where the Lord appeared enthroned upon the cherubim above the mercy-seat. It is doubtful, however, whether the reading of the Hebrew text in either passage is correct. According to the Septuagint the proverb quoted in Genesis should run : " In the mountain is the Lord seen," and the same authority changes the "Moriah" of the Book of Chronicles into *Amôr-eia*, " of the Amorites."

It is true that the distance of Jerusalem from Beer-sheba would agree well with the three days' journey of Abraham. But it is difficult to reconcile the description of the scene of Abraham's sacrifice with the future temple-mount. Where Isaac was bound to the altar was a solitary spot, the patriarch and his son were alone there, and it was overgrown with brushwood so thickly that a ram had been caught in it by his horns. The temple-mount, on the contrary, was either within the walls of a city or just outside them, and the city was already a capital famous for its worship of "the most High God." Had the Moriah of Jerusalem really been the site of Abraham's altar it is strange that no allusion is made to the fact by the writers of the Old Testament, or that tradition should have been silent on the matter. We must be content with the knowledge that it was to one of the mountains "in the land of Moriah" that Abraham was led, and that "Moriah" was a "land," not a single mountain-peak.[1]

Abraham returned to Beer-sheba, and from thence went to Hebron, where Sarah died. Hebron —or Kirjath-Arba as it was then called—was occupied by a Hittite tribe, in contradistinction

---

[1] We should not forget that the Septuagint reads "the highlands," that is, *Moreh* instead of *Moriah*, while the Syriac version boldly changes the word into the name of the "Amorites." For arguments on the other side, see p. 79.

to the country round about it, which was in the possession of the Amorites. As at Jerusalem, or at Kadesh on the Orontes, the Hittites had intruded into Amoritish territory and established themselves in the fortress-town. But while the Hittite city was known as Kirjath-Arba, " the city of Arba," the Amoritish district was named Mamre : the union of Kirjath-Arba and Mamre created the Hebron of a later day.

Kirjath-Arba seems to have been built in the valley, close to the pools which still provide water for its modern inhabitants. On the eastern side the slope of the hill is honeycombed with tombs cut in the rock, and, if ancient tradition is to be believed, it was in one of these that Abraham desired to lay the body of his wife. The "double cave" of Machpelah—for so the Septuagint renders the phrase—was in the field of Ephron the Hittite, and from Ephron, accordingly, the Hebrew patriarch purchased the land for 400 shekels of silver, or about £47. The cave, we are told, lay opposite Mamre, which goes to show that the oak under which Abraham once pitched his tent may not have been very far distant from that still pointed out as the oak of Mamre in the grounds of the Russian hospice. The traditional tomb of Machpelah has been venerated alike by Jew, Christian, and Mohammedan. The church built over it in Byzantine days and restored by the Crusaders to Christian worship has been transformed into a mosque, but its sanctity has remained unchanged.

It stands in the middle of a court, enclosed by a solid wall of massive stones, the lower courses of which were cut and laid in their places in the age of Herod. The fanatical Moslem is unwilling that any but himself should enter the sacred precincts, but by climbing the cliff behind the town it is possible to look down upon the mosque and its sacred enclosure, and see the whole building spread out like a map below the feet.

More than one English traveller has been permitted to enter the mosque, and we are now well acquainted with the details of its architecture. But the rock-cut tomb in which the bodies of the patriarchs are supposed to have lain has never been examined by the explorer. It is probable, however, that were he to penetrate into it he would find nothing to reward his pains. During the long period that Hebron was in Christian hands the cave was more than once visited by the pilgrim. But we look in vain in the records which have come down to us for an account of the relics it has been supposed to contain. Had the mummified corpses of the patriarchs been preserved in it, the fact would have been known to the travellers of the Crusading age.[1]

Like the other tombs in its neighbourhood, the cave of Machpelah has doubtless been opened and despoiled at an early epoch. We know that tombs were violated in Egypt long before the days of Abraham, in spite of the penalties with which such

[1] See the *Zeitschrift des deutschen Palästina-Vereins*, 1895.

188 PATRIARCHAL PALESTINE

acts of sacrilege were visited, and the cupidity of the Canaanite was no less great than that of the Egyptian. The treasures buried with the dead were too potent an attraction, and the robber of the tomb braved for their sake the terrors of both this world and the next.

Abraham now sent his servant to Mesopotamia, to seek there for a wife for his son Isaac from among his kinsfolk at Harran. Rebekah, the sister of Laban, accordingly, was brought to Canaan and wedded to her cousin. Isaac was at the time in the southern desert, encamped at the well of Lahai-roi, near Kadesh. So " Isaac was comforted after his mother's death."

" Then again," we are told, " Abraham took a wife," whose name was Keturah, and by whom he was the forefather of a number of Arabian tribes. They occupied the northern and central parts of the Arabian peninsula, by the side of the Ishmael-ites, and colonized the land of Midian. It is the last we hear of the great patriarch. He died soon afterwards "in a good old age," and was buried at Machpelah along with his wife.

Isaac still dwell at Lahai-roi, and there the twins, Esau and Jacob, were born to him. There, too, he still was when a famine fell upon the land, like " the first famine that was in the days of Abraham." The story of Abraham's dealings with Abimelech of Gerar is repeated in the case of Isaac. Again we hear of Phichol, the captain of Abime-lech's army ; again the wife of the patriarch is described as his sister ; and again his herdsmen strive with those of the king of Gerar over the wells they have dug, and the well of Beer-sheba is made to derive its name from the oaths sworn mutually by Isaac and the king. It is hardly conceivable that history could have so closely repeated itself, that the lives of the king and commander-in-chief of Gerar could have extended over so many years, or that the origin of the name of Beer-sheba would have been so quickly forgotten. Rather we must believe that two narratives have been mingled together, and that the earlier visit of Abraham to Gerar has coloured the story of Isaac's sojourn in the territory of Abimelech. We need not refuse to believe that the servants of Isaac dug wells and wrangled over them with the native herdsmen ; that Beer-sheba should twice have received its name from a repetition of the same event is a different matter. One of the wells—that of Rehoboth—made by Isaac's servants is probably referred to in the Egyptian *Travels of a Mohar*, where it is called Rehoburta.

Isaac was not a wanderer like his father. Lahairoi in the desert, "the valley of Gerar," Beersheba and Hebron, were the places round which his life revolved, and they were all close to one another. There is no trace of his presence in the north of Palestine, and when the prophet Amos (vii. 16) makes Isaac synonymous with the northern kingdom of Israel, there can be no geographical reference in his words. Isaac died

eventually at Hebron, and was buried in the
family tomb of Machpelah.

But long before this happened Jacob had fled
from the well-deserved wrath of his brother to his
uncle Laban at Harran. On his way he had slept
on the rocky ridge of Bethel, and had beheld in
vision the angels of God ascending and descending
the steps of a staircase that led to heaven. The
nature of the ground itself must have suggested the
dream. The limestone rock is fissured into step-
like terraces, which seem formed of blocks of stone
piled one upon the other, and rising upwards like a
gigantic staircase towards the sky. On the hill
that towers above the ruins of Beth-el, we may still
fancy that we see before us the "ladder" of Jacob.

But the vision was more than a mere dream.
God appeared in it to the patriarch, and repeated
to him the promise that had been made to his
fathers. Through Jacob, the younger of the twins,
the true line of Abraham was to be carried on.
When he awoke in the morning the fugitive recognized the real character of his dream. He took,
accordingly, the stone that had served him for a
pillow, and setting it up as an altar, poured oil upon
it, and so made it a Beth-el, or "House of God."
Henceforward it was a consecrated altar, a holy
memorial of the God whose divinity had been
mysteriously imparted to it.

The Semitic world was full of such Beth-els, or
consecrated stones. They are referred to in the
literature of ancient Babylonia, and an English

traveller, Mr. Doughty, has found them still exist-
ing near the Tema of the Old Testament in
Northern Arabia. In Phœnicia we are told that
they abounded. The solitary rock in the desert or
on the mountain-side seemed to the primitive
Semite the dwelling-place of Deity; it rose up
awe-striking and impressive in its solitary grandeur
and venerable antiquity; it was a shelter to him
from the heat of the sun, and a protection from the
perils of the night. When his worship and adora-
tion came in time to be transferred from the stone
itself to the divinity it had begun to symbolize, it
became an altar on which the libation of oil or
wine might be poured out to the gods, and on the
seals of Syria and the sculptured slabs of Assyria
we accordingly find it transformed into a portable
altar, and merged in the cone-like symbol of the
goddess Ashêrah. The stone which had itself been
a Beth-el wherein the Deity had his home, passed
by degrees into the altar of the god whose actual
dwelling-place was in heaven.

The Canaanitish city near which Jacob had
raised the monument of his dream bore the name
of Luz. In Israelitish days, however, the name of
the monument was transferred to that of the city,
and Luz itself was called the Beth-el, or " House of
God." The god worshipped there when the Israelites
first entered Canaan appears to have been entitled
On,—a name derived, perhaps, from that of the
city of the Sun-god in Egypt. Bethel was also
Beth-On, "the temple of On," from whence the

tribe of Benjamin afterwards took the name of Ben-Oni, " the Onite." Beth-On has survived into our own times, and the site of the old city is still known as Beitîn.

It is not needful to follow the adventures of Jacob in Mesopotamia. His new home lay far away from the boundaries of Palestine, and though the kings of Aram-Naharaim made raids at times into the land of Canaan and caused their arms to be feared within the walls of Jerusalem, they never made any permanent conquests on the coasts of the Mediterranean. In the land of the Aramæans Jacob is lost for awhile from the history of patriarchal Palestine.

When he again emerges, it is as a middle-aged man, rich in flocks and herds, who has won two wives as the reward of his labours, and is already the father of a family. He is on his way back to the country which had been promised to his seed and wherein he himself had been born. Laban, his father-in-law, robbed at once of his daughters and his household gods, is pursuing him, and has overtaken him on the spurs of Mount Gilead, almost within sight of his goal. There a covenant is made between the Aramæan and the Hebrew, and a cairn of stones is piled up to commemorate the fact. The cairn continued to bear a double name, the Aramæan name given to it by Laban, and the Canaanitish name of Galeed, " the heap of witnesses," by which it was called by Jacob. The double name was a sign of the two populations and languages which the cairn separated from one another. Northward were the Aramæans and an Aramaic speech; southward the land of Canaan and the language which we term Hebrew.

The spot where the cairn was erected bore yet another title. It was also called Mizpah, the "watch-tower," the outpost from which the dweller in Canaan could discern the approaching bands of an enemy from the north or east. It protected the road to the Jordan, and kept watch over the eastern plateau. Here in after times Jephthah gathered around him the patriots of Israel, and delivered his people from the yoke of the Ammonites.

Once more "Jacob went on his way," and from the "two-fold camp" of Mahanaim sent messengers to his brother Esau, who had already established himself among the mountains of Seir. Then came the mysterious struggle in the silent darkness of night with one whom the patriarch believed to have been his God Himself. When day dawned, the vision departed from him, but not until his name had been changed. "Thy name," it was declared to him, "shall be called no more Jacob, but Israel; for as a prince hast thou power with God and with men, and hast prevailed." And his thigh was shrunken, so that the children of Israel in days to come abstained from eating "of the sinew which shrank, which is upon the hollow of the thigh." The spot where the struggle took place, beside the waters of the Jabbok, was named Penu-el, "the face of God." There was more than

N

one other Penu-el in the Semitic world, and at
Carthage the goddess Tanith was entitled Peni-
Baal, "the face of Baal."

The name of Israel, as we may learn from its
equivalent, Jeshurun, was really derived from a
root which signified "to be straight," or "upright."
The Israelites were in truth "the people of upright-
ness." It is only by one of those plays upon
words, of which the Oriental is still so fond, that
the name can be brought into connection with the
word *sar*, "a prince." But the name of Jacob was
well known among the northern Semites. We
gather from the inscriptions of Egypt that its full
form was Jacob-el. Like Jeshurun by the side of
Israel, or Jephthah by the side of Jiphthah-el (Josh.
xix. 27), Jacob is but an abbreviated Jacob-el.
One of the places in Palestine conquered by the
Pharaoh Thothmes III., the names of which are
recorded on the walls of his temple at Karnak,
was Jacob-el—a reminiscence, doubtless, of the
Hebrew patriarch. Professor Flinders Petrie has
made us acquainted with Egyptian scarabs on
which is inscribed in hieroglyphic characters the
name of a king, Jacob-har or Jacob-hal, who
reigned in the valley of the Nile before Abraham
entered it, and Mr. Pinches has lately discovered
the name of Jacob-el among the persons mentioned in contracts of the time of the Babylonian
sovereign Sin-mu-ballidh, who was a contemporary
of Chedor-laomer. We thus have monumental
evidence that the name of Jacob was well known

in the Semitic world in the age of the Hebrew patriarchs.

Jacob and Esau met and were reconciled, and Jacob then journeyed onwards to Succoth, "the booths." The site of this village of "booths" is unknown, but it could not have been far from the banks of the Jordan and the road to Nablûs. The neighbourhood of Shechem, called in Greek times Neapolis, the Nablûs of to-day, was the next resting-place of the patriarch. If we are to follow the translation of the Authorised Version, it would have been at "Shalem, a city of Shechem," that his tents were pitched. But many eminent scholars believe that the Hebrew words should rather be rendered : "And Jacob came in peace to the city of Shechem," the reference being to his peaceable parting from his brother. There is, however, a hamlet still called Salîm, nearly three miles to the east of Nablûs, and it may be therefore that it was really at a place termed Shalem that Jacob rested on his way. In this case the field bought from Hamor, "before the city of Shechem," cannot have been where, since the days of our Lord, "Jacob's well" has been pointed out (S. John iv. 5, 6). The well is situated considerably westward of Salîm, midway, in fact, between that village and Nablûs, and close to the village of 'Askâr, with which the "Sychar" of S. John's Gospel has sometimes been identified. It has been cut through the solid rock to a depth of more than a hundred feet, and the groovings made by the ropes of the waterpots in far-off centuries are still visible at its mouth. But no water can be drawn from it now. The well is choked with the rubbish of a ruined church, built above it in the early days of Christianity, and of which all that remains is a broken arch. It has been dug at a spot where the road from Shechem to the Jordan branches off from that which runs towards the north, though Shechem itself is more than a mile distant. We should notice that S. John does not say that the well was actually in "the parcel of ground that Jacob gave to his son Joseph," only that it was "near to" the patriarch's field.

If Jacob came to Shechem in peace, the peace was of no long continuance. Simeon and Levi, the sons of the patriarch, avenged the insult offered by the Shechemite prince to their sister Dinah, by treacherously falling upon the city and slaying "all the males." Jacob was forced to fly, leaving behind him the altar he had erected. He made for the Canaanitish city of Luz, the Beth-el of later days, where he had seen the great altar-stairs sloping upward to heaven. The idols that had been carried from Mesopotamia were buried "under the oak which was by Shechem," along with the ear-rings of the women. The oak was one of those sacred trees which abounded in the Semitic world, like another oak at Beth-el, beneath which the nurse of Rebekah was soon afterwards to be buried.

At Beth-el Jacob built another altar. But he

could not rest there, and once more took his way to the south. On the road his wife Rachel died while giving birth to his youngest son, and her tomb beside the path to Beth-lehem was marked by a "pillar" which the writer of the Book of Genesis tells us remained to his own day. It indicated the boundary between the territories of Benjamin and Judah at Zelzah (1 Sam. x. 2).

At Beth-lehem Jacob lingered a long while. His flocks and herds were spread over the country, under the charge of his sons, browsing on the hills and watered at the springs, for which the "hill-country of Judah" was famous. In their search for pasturage they wandered northward, we are told, "beyond the tower of the Flock," which guarded the Jebusite stronghold of Zion (Mic. iv. 8). Beth-lehem itself was more commonly known in that age by the name of Ephrath. Beth-lehem, "the temple of Lehem," must, in fact, have been the sacred name of the city derived from the worship of its chief deity, and Mr. Tomkins is doubtless right in seeing in this deity the Babylonian Lakhmu, who with his consort Lakhama, was regarded as a primæval god of the nascent world.

At Beth-lehem Jacob was but a few miles distant from Hebron, where Isaac still lived, and where at his death he was buried by his sons Jacob and Esau in the family tomb of Machpelah. It was the last time, seemingly, that the two brothers found themselves together. Esau, partly by marriage, partly by conquest, dispossessed the Horites of Mount Seir, and founded the kingdom of Edom, while the sons and flocks of Jacob scattered themselves from Hebron in the south of Canaan to Shechem in its centre. The two hallowed sanctuaries of the future kingdoms of Judah and Israel, where the first throne was set up in Israel and the monarchy of David was first established, thus became the boundaries of the herdsmen's domain. In both the Hebrew patriarch held ground that was rightfully his own. It was a sign that the house of Israel should hereafter occupy the land which the family of Israel thus roamed over with their flocks. The nomad was already passing into the settler, with fields and burial-places of his own.

But before the transformation could be fully accomplished, a long season of growth and preparation was needful. Egypt, and not Canaan, was to be the land in which the Chosen People should be trained for their future work. Canaan itself was to pass under Egyptian domination, and to replace the influence of Babylonian culture by that of Egypt. It was a new world and a new civilization into which the descendants of Jacob were destined to emerge when finally they escaped from the fiery furnace of Egyptian bondage. The Egypt known to Jacob was an Egypt over which Asiatic princes ruled, and whose vizier was himself a Hebrew. It was the Egypt of the Hyksos conquerors, whose capital was Zoan, on the frontiers of Asia, and whose people were the slaves of an Asiatic stranger. The Egypt quitted by his descendants was one which had subjected Asia to itself, and had carried the spoils of Syria to its splendid capital in the far south. The Asiatic wave had been rolled back from the banks of the Nile, and Egyptian conquest and culture had overflooded Asia as far as the Euphrates.

But it was not Egypt alone which had undergone a change. The Canaan of Abraham and Jacob looked to Babylonia for its civilization, its literature, and its laws. Its princes recognized at times the supremacy of the Babylonian sovereigns, and the deities of Babylonia were worshipped in its midst. The Canaan of Moses had long been a province of the Egyptian Empire; Egyptian rule had been substituted for that of Babylon, and the manners and customs of Egypt had penetrated deeply into the minds of its inhabitants. The Hittite invasion from the north had blocked the high-road to Babylonia, and diverted the trade of Palestine towards the west and the south. While Abraham, the native of Ur, and the emigrant from Harran, had found himself in Canaan, and even at Zoan, still within the sphere of the influences among which he had grown up, the fugitives from Egypt entered on the invasion of a country which had but just been delivered from the yoke of the Pharaohs. It was an Egyptian Canaan that the Israelites were called upon to subdue, and it was fitting therefore that they should have been made ready for the task by their long sojourn in the land of Goshen.

How that sojourn came about, it is not for us to recount. The story of Joseph is too familiar to be repeated, though we are but just beginning to learn how true it is, in all its details, to the facts which Egyptian research is bringing more and more fully to light. We see the Midianite and Ishmaelite caravan passing Dothan — still known by its ancient name—with their bales of spicery from Gilead for the dwellers in the Delta, and carrying away with them the young Hebrew slave. We watch his rise in the house of his Egyptian master, his wrongful imprisonment and sudden exaltation when he sits by the side of Pharaoh and governs Egypt in the name of the king. We read the pathetic story of the old father sending his sons to buy corn from the royal granaries or *larits* of Egypt, and withholding to the last his youngest and dearest one ; of the Beduin shepherds bowing all unconsciously before the brother whom they had sold into slavery, and who now holds in his hands the power of life and death ; of Joseph's disclosure of himself to the conscious-stricken suppliants ; of Jacob's cry when convinced at last that "the governor over all the land of Egypt" was his long-mourned son. "It is enough ; Joseph my son is yet alive : I will go and see him before I die."

Jacob and his family travelled in wagons along the high-road which connected the south of Palestine with the Delta. It led past Beer-sheba and El-Arîsh to the Shur, or line of fortifications which protected the eastern frontier of Egypt. The modern caravan road follows its course most of the way. It was thus distinct from "the way of the Philistines," which led along the coast of the Mediterranean, on the northern edge of the Sirbonian Lake. In Egypt the Israelitish emigrants settled not far from the Hyksos capital in the land of Goshen, which the excavations of Dr. Naville have shown to be the Wâdi Tumilât of to-day. Here they multiplied and grew wealthy, until the evil days came when the Egyptians rose up against Semitic influence and control, and Ramses II. transformed the free-born Beduin into public serfs.

But the age of Ramses II. was still far distant when Jacob died full of years, and his mummy was carried to the burial-place of his fathers "in the land of Canaan." Local tradition connected the name of Abel-mizraim, "the meadow of Egypt," on the eastern side of the Jordan, with the long funeral procession which wended its way from Zoan to Hebron. We cannot believe, however, that the mourners would have so far gone out of their road, even if the etymology assigned by tradition to the name could be supported. The tradition bears witness to the fact of the procession, but to nothing more.

With the funeral of Jacob a veil falls upon the Biblical history of Canaan, until the days when the spies were sent out to search the land. Joseph was buried in Egypt, not at Hebron, though he had made the Israelites swear before his death that his mummy should be eventually taken to Palestine. The road to Hebron, it is clear, was no longer open, and the power of the Hyksos princes must have been fast waning. The war of independence had broken out, and the native kings of Upper Egypt were driving the foreigner back into Asia. The rulers of Zoan had no longer troops to spare for a funeral procession through the eastern desert.

The Chronicler, however, has preserved a notice which seems to show that a connection was still kept up between Southern Canaan and the Hebrew settlers in Goshen, even after Jacob's death, perhaps while he was yet living. We are told that certain of the sons of Ephraim were slain by the men of Gath, whose cattle they had attempted to steal, and that their father, after mourning many days, comforted himself with the birth of other sons (1 Chron. vii. 21—26). The notice, moreover, does not stand alone. Thothmes III., the great conqueror of the eighteenth Egyptian dynasty, states that two of the places captured by him in Palestine were Jacob-el and Joseph-el. It is tempting to see in the two names reminiscences of the Hebrew patriarch and his son. If so, the name of Joseph would have been impressed upon a locality in Canaan more than two centuries before the Exodus. The geographical lists of Thothmes

III. and the fragments of early history preserved by the Chronicler would thus support and complete one another. The Egyptian cavalry who accompanied the mummy of Jacob to its resting-place at Machpelah, would not be the only evidence of the authority claimed by Joseph and his master in the land of Canaan ; Joseph himself would have left his name there, and his grand-children would have fought against " the men of Gath."

But these are speculations which may, or may not, be confirmed by archæological discovery. For the Book of Genesis Canaan disappears from sight with the death of Jacob. Henceforward it is upon Egypt and the nomad settlers in Goshen that the attention of the Pentateuch is fixed, until the time comes when the age of the patriarchs is superseded by that of the legislator, and Moses, the adopted son of the Egyptian princess, leads his people back to Canaan. Joseph had been carried by Midianitish hands out of Palestine into Egypt, there to become the representative of the Pharaoh, and son-in-law of the high-priest of Heliopolis ; for Moses, the adopted grandson of the Pharaoh, "learned in all the wisdom of the Egyptians," it was reserved, after years of trial and preparation in Midian, to bring the descendants of Jacob out of their Egyptian prison-house to the borders of the Promised Land.

CHAPTER V

EGYPTIAN TRAVELLERS IN CANAAN

PALESTINE has been a land of pilgrims and tourists from the very beginning of its history. It was the goal of the migration of Abraham and his family, and it was equally the object of the oldest book of travels with which we are acquainted. Allusion has already been made more than once to the Egyptian papyrus, usually known as *The Travels of a Mohar*, and in which a satirical account is given of a tour in Palestine and Syria. The writer was a professor, apparently of literature, in the court of Ramses II., and he published a series of letters to his friend, Nekht-sotep, which were long admired as models of style. Nekht-sotep was one of the secretaries attached to the military staff, and among the letters is a sort of parody of an account given by Nekht-sotep of his adventures in Canaan, which was intended partly to show how an account of the kind ought to have been written by an accomplished penman, partly to prove the superiority of the scribe's life to that of the soldier, partly also, it may be, for the sake of teasing the

writer's correspondent.   Nekht-sotep had evidently
assumed airs of superiority on the strength of his
foreign travels, and his stay-at-home friend undertook to demonstrate that he had himself enjoyed
the more comfortable life of the two.   Nekht-sotep
is playfully dubbed with the foreign title of Mohar
—or more correctly Muhir—a word borrowed from
Assyrian, where it primarily signified a military
commander and then the governor of a province.

Long before the days of the nineteenth dynasty,
however, there had been Egyptian travellers in
Palestine, or at least in the adjoining countries.
One of the Egyptian books which have come down
to us contains the story of a certain Sinuhit who
had to fly from Egypt in consequence of some
political troubles in which he was involved after
the death of Amon-m-hat I. of the twelfth dynasty.
Crossing the Nile near Kher-ahu, the Old Cairo of
to-day, he gained the eastern bank of the river and
made his way to the line of forts which protected
Egypt from its Asiatic enemies.   Here he crouched
among the desert bushes till night-fall, lest "the
watchmen of the tower" should see him, and then
pursued his journey under the cover of darkness.
At daybreak he reached the land of Peten and
the wadi of Qem-uer on the line of the modern
Suez Canal.   There thirst seized upon him ; his
throat rattled, and he said to himself—"This is
the taste of death."   A Bedawi, however, perceived
him and had compassion on the fugitive : he gave
him water and boiled milk, and Sinuhit for a while

joined the nomad tribe. Then he passed on to the country of Qedem, the Kadmonites of the Old Testament (Gen. xv. 19 ; Judges vi. 3), whence came the wise men of the East (1 Kings iv. 30). After spending a year and a half there, 'Ammu-anshi, the prince of the Upper land of Tenu, asked the Egyptian stranger to come to him, telling him that he would hear the language of Egypt. He added that he had already heard about Sinuhit from "the Egyptians who were in the country." It is clear from this that there had been intercourse for some time between Egypt and "the Upper Tenu."

It is probable that Dr. W. Max Müller is right in seeing in Tenu an abbreviated form of Lutennu (or Rutenu), the name by which Syria was known to the Egyptians. There was an Upper Lutennu and a Lower Lutennu, the Upper Lutennu corresponding with Palestine and the adjoining country, and thus including the Edomite district of which 'Ammu-anshi or Ammi-anshi was king.· In the name of 'Ammu-anshi, it may be observed, we have the name of the deity who appears as Ammi or Ammon in the kingdom of the Ammonites, and perhaps forms the second element in the name of Balaam. The same divine name enters into the composition of those of early kings of Ma'in in Southern Arabia, as well as of Babylonia in the far East.[1]

'Ammu-anshi married Sinuhit to his eldest daughter, and bestowed upon him the government

[1] See above, p. 64.

of a district called Aia which lay on the frontier of a neighbouring country. Aia is described as rich in vines, figs, and olives, in wheat and barley, in milk and cattle. "Its wine was more plentiful than water," and Sinuhit had "daily rations of bread and wine, cooked meat and roast fowl," as well as abundance of game. He lived there for many years. The children born to him by his Asiatic wife grew up and became heads of tribes. "I gave water to the thirsty," he says; "I set on his journey the traveller who had been hindered from passing by; I chastised the brigand. I commanded the Beduin who departed afar to strike and repel the princes of foreign lands, and they marched (under me), for the prince of Tenu allowed that I should be during long years the general of his soldiers."

Sinuhit, in fact, had given proof of his personal prowess at an early period in his career. The champion of Tenu had come to him in his tent and challenged him to single combat. The Egyptian was armed with bow, arrows, and dagger; his adversary with battle-axe, javelins, and buckler. The contest was short, and ended in the decisive victory of Sinuhit, who wounded his rival and despoiled him of his goods.

A time came, however, when Sinuhit grew old, and began to long to see once more the land of his fathers before he died. Accordingly he sent a petition to the Pharaoh praying him to forgive the offences of his youth and allow him to return again to Egypt. The petition was granted, and a letter was despatched to the refugee, permitting him to return. Sinuhit accordingly quitted the land where he had lived so long. First of all he held a festival, and handed over his property to his children, making his eldest son the chief of the tribe. Then he travelled southward to Egypt, and was graciously received at court. The coarse garments of the Beduin were exchanged for fine linen; his body was bathed with water and scented essences; he lay once more on a couch and enjoyed the luxurious cookery of the Egyptians. A house and pyramid were built for him; a garden was laid out for him with a lake and a kiosk, and a golden statue with a robe of electrum was set up in it. Sinuhit ceased to be an Asiatic "barbarian," and became once more a civilized Egyptian.

The travels of Sinuhit were involuntary, but a time came when a tour in Palestine was almost as much the fashion as it is to-day. The conquests of Thothmes III. had made Syria an Egyptian province, and had introduced Syrians into the Egyptian bureaucracy. Good roads were made throughout the newly-acquired territory, furnished with post-houses where food and lodging could be procured, and communication between Egypt and Canaan thus became easy and frequent. The fall of the eighteenth dynasty caused only a momentary break in the intercourse between the two countries; with the establishment of the nineteenth dynasty it was again resumed. Messengers passed backward and forward between Syria and the court of the Pharaoh; Asiatics once more thronged into the valley of the Nile, and the Egyptian civil servant and traveller followed in the wake of the victorious armies of Seti and Ramses. *The Travels of a Mohar* is the result of this renewed acquaintance with the cities and roads of Palestine.

The writer is anxious to display his knowledge of Syrian geography. Though he had not himself ventured to brave the discomforts of foreign travel, he wished to show that he knew as much about Canaan as those who had actually been there. A tour there was after all not much to boast of; it had become so common that the geography of Canaan was as well known as that of Egypt itself, and the stay-at-home scribe had consequently no difficulty in compiling a guide-book to it.

The following is the translation given by Dr. Brugsch of the papyrus, with such alterations as have been necessitated by further study and research. "I will portray for thee the likeness of a Mohar, I will let thee know what he does. Hast thou not gone to the land of the Hittites, and hast thou not seen the land of Aupa? Dost thou not know what Khaduma is like; the land of Igad'i also how it is formed? The Zar (or Plain) of king Sesetsu (Sesostris)—on which side of it lies the town of Aleppo, and how is its ford? Hast thou not taken thy road to Kadesh (on the Orontes) and Tubikhi? Hast thou not gone to the Shasu (Beduin) with numerous mercenaries, and hast thou not trodden the way to the Maghar[at] (the caves of the

O

Magoras near Beyrout) where the heaven is dark in the daytime? The place is planted with maple-trees, oaks, and acacias, which reach up to heaven, full of beasts, bears (?), and lions, and surrounded by Shasu in all directions. Hast thou not ascended the mountain of Shaua, and hast thou not trodden it? There thy hands hold fast to the [rein] of thy chariot; a jerk has shaken thy horses in drawing it. I pray thee, let us go to the city of Beeroth (Beyrout). Hast thou not hastened to its ascent after passing over the ford in front of it?

"Do thou explain this relish for [the life of] a Mohar! Thy chariot lies there [before] thee; thy [feet] have fallen lame; thou treadest the backward path at eventide. All thy limbs are ground small. Thy [bones] are broken to pieces, and thou dost fall asleep. Thou awakest: it is the time of gloomy night, and thou art alone. Has not a thief come to rob thee? Some grooms have entered the stable; the horse kicks out; the thief has made off in the night, thy clothes are stolen. Thy groom wakes up in the night; he sees what has happened to him; he takes what is left, he goes off to bad company, he joins the Beduin. He transforms himself into an Asiatic. The police (?) come, they [feel about] for the robber; he is discovered, and is immovable from terror. Thou wakest, thou findest no trace of them, for they have carried off thy property.

"Become [again] a Mohar who is fully accoutred.

Let thy ear be filled with that which I relate to thee besides.

"The town ' Hidden '—such is the meaning of its name Gebal—what is its condition? Its goddess [we will speak of] at another time. Hast thou not visited it? Be good enough to look out for Beyrout, Sidon, and Sarepta. Where are the fords of the land of Nazana? The country of Authu (Usu), what is its condition? They are situated above another city in the sea, Tyre the port is its name. Drinking-water is brought to it in boats. It is richer in fishes than in sand. I will tell thee of something else. It is dangerous to enter Zair'aun. Thou wilt say it is burning with a very painful sting (?). Come, Mohar. Go forward on the way to the land of Pa-'A . . ina. Where is the road to Achshaph (Ekdippa)? Towards which town? Pray look at the mountain of User. How is its crest? Where is the mountain of Sakama (Shechem)? Who can surmount it? Mohar, whither must you take a journey to the land of Hazor? How is its ford? Show me how one goes to Hamath, Dagara, [and] Dagar-el, to the place where all Mohars meet? Be good enough to spy out its road; cast a look on Yâ . . . When one goes to the land of Adamim, to what is one opposite? Do not draw back, but instruct us. Guide us, that we may know, O leader!

"I will name to thee other cities besides these. Hast thou not gone to the land of Takhis, to Kafir-Marona, Tamnah, Kadesh, Dapul, Azai, Har-nammata, and hast thou not seen Kirjath-Anab, near Beth-Sopher? and dost thou not know Adullam [and] Zidiputa? Or dost thou not know any better the name of Khalza in the land of Aupa, [like] a bull upon its frontiers? Here is the place where all the mighty warriors are seen. Be good enough to look and see the chapel of the land of Qina, and tell me about Rehob. Describe Bethsha-el (Beth-el) along with Tarqa-el. The ford of the land of Jordan, how is it crossed? Teach me to know the passage that leads to the land of Megiddo, which lies in front of it. Verily thou art a Mohar, well skilled in the work of the strong hand. Pray, is there found a Mohar like thee, to place at the head of the army, or a *seigneur* who can beat thee in shooting?

" Beware of the gorge of the precipice, 2000 cubits deep, which is full of rocks and boulders. Thou turnest back in a zigzag, thou bearest thy bow, thou takest the iron in thy left hand. Thou lettest the old men see, if their eyes are good, how, worn out with fatigue, thou supportest thyself with thy hand. *Ebed gamal Mohar n'amu* ('A camel's slave is the Mohar! they say'); so they say, and thou gainest a name among the Mohars and the knights of the land of Egypt. Thy name becomes like that of Qazairnai, the lord of Asel, when the lions found him in the thicket, in the defile which is rendered dangerous by the Shasu who lie in ambush among the trees. They measured four cubits from the nose to the heel, they had a grim look, without softness; they cared not for caresses.

"Thou art alone, no strong one is with thee, no *armée* is behind thee, no *Ariel* who prepares the way for thee, and gives thee information of the road before thee. Thou knowest not the road. The hair on thy head stands on end; it bristles up. Thy soul is given into thy hands. Thy path is full of rocks and boulders, there is no outlet near, it is overgrown with creepers and wolf's-bane. The precipice is on one side of thee, the mountain and the wall of rock on the other. Thou drivest in against it. The chariot jumps on which thou art. Thou art troubled to hold up thy horses. If it falls down the precipice, the pole drags thee down too. Thy *ceintures* are pulled away. They fall down. Thou shacklest the horse, because the pole is broken on the path of the defile. Not knowing how to tie it up, thou understandest not how it is to be repaired. The *essieu* is left on the spot, as the load is too heavy for the horses. Thy courage has evaporated. Thou beginnest to run. The heaven is cloudless. Thou art thirsty; the enemy is behind thee; a trembling seizes thee; a twig of thorny acacia worries thee; thou thrustest it aside; the horse is scratched till at length thou findest rest.

"Explain to me thy liking for [the life of] a Mohar!

"Thou comest into Joppa; thou findest the date-palm in full bloom in its time. Thou openest wide thy mouth in order to eat. Thou findest that the maid who keeps the garden is fair. She does whatever thou wantest of her. . . Thou art recognized, thou art brought to trial, and owest thy preservation to being a Mohar. Thy girdle of the finest stuff thou payest as the price of a worthless rag. Thou sleepest every evening with a rug of fur over thee. Thou sleepest a deep sleep, for thou art weary. A thief steals thy bow and thy sword from thy side; thy quiver and thy armour are cut to pieces in the darkness; thy pair of horses run away. The groom takes his course over a slippery path which rises before him. He breaks thy chariot in pieces; he follows thy footsteps. [He finds] thy equipments which had fallen on the ground and had sunk into the sand, leaving only an empty space.

" Prayer does not avail thee, even when thy mouth says, 'Give food in addition to water, that I may reach my goal in safety,' they are deaf and will not hear. They say not yes to thy words. The iron-workers enter into the smithy; they rummage in the workshops of the carpenters; the handicraftsmen and saddlers are at hand; they do whatever thou requirest. They put together thy chariot; they put aside the parts of it that are made useless; thy spokes are *façonné* quite new; thy wheels are put on; they put the *courroies* on the axles and on the hinder part; they splice thy yoke, they put on the box of thy chariot; the [workmen] in iron forge the . . . ; they put the ring that is wanting on thy whip, they replace the *lanières* upon it.

"Thou goest quickly onward to fight on the battle-field, to do the deeds of a strong hand and of firm courage.

"Before I wrote I sought me out a Mohar who knows his power and leads the *jeunesse*, a chief in the *armée*, [who travels] even to the end of the world.

"Answer me not 'This is good; this is bad;' repeat not to me your opinion. Come, I will tell thee all that lies before thee at the end of thy journey.

"I begin for thee with the palace of Sesetsu (Sesostris). Hast thou not set foot in it by force? Hast thou not eaten the fish in the brook . . . ? Hast thou not washed thyself in it? With thy permission I will remind thee of Huzana; where is its fortress? Come, I pray thee, to the palace of the land of Uazit, even of Osymandyas (Ramses II.) in his victories, [to] S . . z-el, together with Absaqbu. I will inform thee of the land of 'Ainin (the two Springs), the customs of which thou knowest not. The land of the lake of Nakhai, and the land of Rehoburta thou hast not seen since thou wast born, O Mohar. Rapih is widely extended. What is its wall like? It extends for a mile in the direction of Gaza."

The French words introduced from time to time by Dr. Brugsch into the translation represent the Semitic words which the Egyptian writer has employed. They illustrate the fashionable tendency of his day to fill the Egyptian vocabulary with the words and phrases of Canaan. It was the revenge taken by Palestine for its invasion and conquest by the armies of Seti and Ramses. Thus *armée* corresponds to the Semitic *tsaba*, "army," *jeunesse* to *na'aruna*, "young men." The Egyptian scribe, however, sometimes made mistakes similar to those which modern novelists are apt to commit in their French quotations. Instead of writing, as he intended, *'ebed gamal Mohar na'amu* ("a camel's slave is the Mohar! they say"), he has assigned the Canaanite vowel *ayin* to the wrong word, and mis-spelt the name of the "camel," so that the phrase is transformed into *abad kamal Mohar n'amu* ("the camel of the Mohar has perished, they are pleasant").[1]

Most of the geographical names mentioned in the papyrus can be identified. Aupa, the Ubi of the Tel el-Amarna tablets, was on the borders of the land of the Hittites, and not far from Aleppo. The Zar or "Plain" of Sesostris makes its appearance in the lists of conquered towns and countries which were drawn up by Thothmes III., Seti I., Ramses II., and Ramses III., in order to commemorate their victories in Syria. The word probably migrated from Babylonia, where the *zeru*

---

[1] It is curious that a similar mistake in regard to the spelling of *'ebed*, "slave" or "servant," has been made in an Aramaic inscription which I have discovered on the rocks near Silsileh in Upper Egypt, where the name of Ebed-Nebo is written Abed-Nebo.

denoted the alluvial plain which lay between the Tigris and the Euphrates. Kadesh, the southern capital of the Hittites, "in the land of the Amorites," lay on the Orontes, close to the lake of Homs, and has been identified by Major Conder with the modern Tel em-Mindeh. Tubikhi, of which we have already heard in the Tel el-Amarna letters, is also mentioned in the geographical lists inscribed by Thothmes III. on the walls of his temple at Karnak (No. 6); it there precedes the name of Kamta or Qamdu, the Kumidi of Tel el-Amarna. It is the Tibhath of the Old Testament, out of which David took "very much brass" (1 Chron. xviii. 8). The Maghar(at) or "Caves" gave their name to the Magoras, the river of Beyrout, as well as to the Mearah of the Book of Joshua (xiii. 4). As for the mountain of Shaua, it is described by the Assyrian king Tiglath-pileser III. as in the neighbourhood of the northern Lebanon, while the city of the Beeroth or "Cisterns" is probably Beyrout.

The Mohar is now carried to Phœnicia. Gebal, Beyrout, Sidon, and Sarepta, are named one after the other, as the traveller is supposed to be journeying from north to south. The "goddess" of Gebal was Baaltis, so often referred to in the letters of Rib-Hadad, who calls her "the mistress of Gebal." In saying, however, that the name of the city meant "Hidden," the writer has been misled by the Egyptian mispronunciation of it. It became Kapuna in the mouths of his countrymen, and since *kapu* in Egyptian signified "hidden mystery," he jumped to the conclusion that such was also the etymology of the Phœnician word. In the "fords of the land of Nazana" we must recognize the river Litâny, which flows into the sea between Sarepta and Tyre. At all events, Authu or Usu, the next city mentioned, is associated with Tyre both in the tablets of Tel el-Amarna and in the inscriptions of the Assyrian kings. It seems to have been the Palætyros or "Older Tyre" of classical tradition, which stood on the mainland opposite the more famous insular Tyre. Phœnician tradition ascribes its foundation to Usôos, the offspring of the mountains of Kasios and Lebanon, and brother of Memrumus, "the exalted," and Hypsouranios, "the lord of heaven," who was the first to invent a clothing of skins, and to sail upon the water in boats, and who had taught mankind to adore the fire and the winds, and to set up two pillars of stone in honour of the deity. From Usu the Mohar is naturally taken to the island rock of Tyre.

Next comes a name which it is difficult to identify. All that is clear is that between Zar or Tyre and Zair'aun there is some connection both of name and of locality. Perhaps Dr. Brugsch is right in thinking that in the next sentence there is a play upon the Hebrew word *zir'âh*, "hornet," which seems to have the same root as Zair'aun. It may be that Zair'aun is the ancient city south of Tyre whose ruins are now called Umm el-'Amûd, and whose older name is said to have been Turân. Unfortunately the name of the next place referred to in the Mohar's travels is doubtful; if it is Pa-'A(y)ina, "the Spring," we could identify it with the modern Râs el-'Ain, "the Head of the Spring." This is on the road to Zîb, the ancient Achshaph or Ekdippa.

"The mountain of User" reminds us curiously of the tribe of Asher, whose territory included the mountain-range which rose up behind the Phœnician coast. But it may denote Mount Carmel, whose "crest" faces the traveller as he makes his way southward from Tyre and Zîb. In any case the allusion to it brings to the writer's mind another mountain in the same neighbourhood, the summit of which similarly towers into the sky. This is "the mountain of Shechem," either Ebal or Gerizim, each of which is nearly 3000 feet above the level of the sea. It is the first mention that we have of Shechem outside the pages of the Old Testament.

Shechem, however, did not lie in the path of the Mohar, and the reference to its mountain is made parenthetically only. We are therefore carried on to Hazor, which afterwards became a city of Naphtali, and of which we hear in the letters of Tel el-Amarna. From Hazor the road ran northwards to Hamath, the Hamah of to-day. Hazor lay not far to the westward of Adamim, which the geographical lists of Thothmes III. place between the Sea of Galilee and the Kishon, and which is doubtless the Adami of Naphtali (Josh. xix. 33). Here the tour of the Mohar comes to an abrupt close. After this the writer contents himself with naming a number of Syrian cities without regard to their geographical position. He is anxious merely to show off his knowledge of Canaanitish geography; perhaps also to insinuate doubts as to the extent of his correspondent's travels.

Takhis, the Thahash of Gen. xxii. 24, was, as we have seen, in the land of the Amorites, not very far distant from Kadesh on the Orontes. Kafir-Marona, "the village of Marona," may have been in the same direction. The second element in the name is met with elsewhere in Palestine. Thus one of Joshua's antagonists was the king of Shim-ron-meron (Josh. xii. 20), and the Assyrian inscriptions tell us of a town called Samsi-muruna. Tamnah was not an uncommon name. We hear of a Tamnah or Timnah in Judah (Josh. xv. 57), and of another in Mount Ephraim (Josh. xix. 50). Dapul may be the Tubuliya of the letters of Rib-Hadad, Azai, "the outlet," seems to have been near a pass, while Har-nammata, "the mountain of Nammata," is called Har-nam by Ramses III., who associates it with Lebanoth and Hebron. The two next names, Kirjath-Anab and Beth-Sopher, are of peculiar interest, since they contain the first mention that has come down to us of Kirjath-Sepher, the literary centre of the Canaanites in the south of Palestine, which was captured and destroyed by Othniel the Kenizzite. In the Old

Testament (Josh. xv. 49, 50) Kirjath-Sannah or Kirjath-Sepher and Anab are coupled together just as Kirjath-Anab and Beth-Sopher are by the Egyptian scribe, and it is therefore evident that he has interchanged the place of the equivalent terms Kirjath, "city," and Beth, "house." But his spelling of the second name shows us how it ought to be punctuated and read in the Old Testament. It was not Kirjath-Sepher, "the city of book(s)," but Kirjath-Sopher, "the city of scribe(s)," and Dr. W. Max Müller has pointed out that the determinative of "writing" has been attached to the word *Sopher*, showing that the writer was fully acquainted with its meaning. Kirjath-Sannah, "the city of instruction," as it was also called, was but another way of emphasizing the fact that here was the site of a library and school such as existed in the towns of Babylonia and Assyria. Both names, however, Kirjath-Sopher and Kirjath-Sannah, were descriptive rather than original; its proper designation seems to have been Debir, "the sanctuary," the temple wherein its library was established, and which has caused the Egyptian author to call it a "Beth," or "temple," instead of a "Kirjath," or "city."

Like Anab and Kirjath-Sopher, Adullam and Zidiputa were also in southern Canaan. It was in the cave of Adullam that David took refuge from the pursuit of Saul, and we learn from Shishak that Zidiputa—or Zadiputh-el, as he calls it—was in the south of Judah. From hence we are suddenly transported to the northern part of Syria, and the Mohar is asked if he knows anything about Khalza in the land of Aupa. Khalza is an Assyrian word signifying "Fortress," and Aupa, the Ubi of the Tel el-Amarna tablets, was not far from Aleppo. The allusion to the "bull" is obscure.

Then once more we are summoned back to Palestine. In the annals of Thothmes III. we are told that "the brook of Qina" was to the south of Megiddo, so that the name of the district has probably survived in that of "Cana of Galilee." Rehob may be Rehob in Asher (Josh. xix. 28), which was near Kanah, though the name is so common in Syria as to make any identification uncertain. Beth-sha-el, on the contrary, is Beth-el. We first meet with the name in the geographical lists of Thothmes III., and the fact that it is Babylonian in form, Bit-sa-ili being the Babylonian equivalent of the Hebrew Beth-el, is one of many proofs that the lists were compiled from a cuneiform original. The name of Beth-sha-el or Beth-el calls up that of Tarqa-el, which contains the name of the Hittite god Tarqu. But where Tarqa-el was situated it is impossible to say.

Towards the end of the book reference is made to certain places which lay on the road between Egypt and Canaan. Rapih is the Raphia of classical geography, the Rapikh of the Assyrian inscriptions, where two broken columns now mark the boundary between Egypt and Turkey. Rehoburta is probably the Rehoboth where the herdsmen of Isaac dug a well before the patriarch moved to Beer-sheba (Gen. xxvi. 22), while in the lake of Nakhai we may have the Sirbonian lake of classical celebrity.

There still remain two allusions in the papyrus which must not be passed over in silence. One is the allusion to " Qazairnai, the lord of Asel," the famous slayer of lions. We know nothing further about this Nimrod of Syria, but Professor Maspero is doubtless right in believing that Asel ought to be written Alsa, and that the country meant was the kingdom of Alasiya, which lay in the northern portion of Cœle-Syria. Several letters from the king of Alasiya are preserved in the Tel el-Amarna collection, and we gather from them that his possessions extended across the Orontes from the desert to the Mediterranean Sea. Egyptian papyri tell us that mares were imported into Egypt from Alasiya as well as two different kinds of liquor. In the age of Samuel and Saul Alasiya was governed by a queen.

The second allusion is to the ironsmith in Canaan. It is clear that there were many of them, and that it was to the worker in iron and not to the worker in bronze that the traveller naturally turned when his chariot needed mending. Even the word that is employed to denote the metal is the Canaanitish *barzel*, which has been adopted under the form of *parzal*. Nothing could show more plainly how characteristic of Canaan the trade of the ironsmith must have been, and how largely the use of iron must have there superseded the use of bronze. The fact is in accordance with the'references in the annals of Thothmes III. to the iron that was received by him from Syria ; it is also in accordance with the statements of the Bible, where we read of the " chariots of iron " in which the Canaanites rode to war. Indeed there seems to have been a special class of wandering ironsmiths in Palestine, like the wandering ironsmiths of mediæval Europe, who jealously guarded the secrets of their trade, and formed not only a peculiar caste, but even a peculiar race. The word Kain means " a smith," and the nomad Kenites of whom we read in the Old Testament were simply the nomad race of "smiths," whose home was the tent or cavern. Hence it was that while they were not Israelites, they were just as little Canaanites, and hence it was too that the Philistines were able to deprive the Israelites of the services of a smith (1 Sam. xiii. 19). All that was necessary was to prevent the Kenites from settling within Israelitish territory. There was no Israelite who knew the secrets of the profession and could take their place, and the Canaanites who lived under Israelitish protection were equally ignorant of the ironsmith's art. Though the ironsmith had made himself a home in Canaan he never identified himself with its inhabitants. The Kenites remained a separate people, and could consequently be classed as such by the side of the Hivites, or " villagers," and the Perizzites, or " fellahin."

If the *Travels of a Mohar* are a guide-book to the geography of Palestine in the age of the nineteenth Egyptian dynasty, the lists of places conquered by Thothmes III., and engraved by his orders on the walls of his temple at Karnak, are a sort of atlas of Canaanite geography in the age of the eighteenth dynasty. The name of each locality is enclosed in a cartouche and surmounted by the head and shoulders of a Canaanitish captive. The hair and eyes of the figures are painted black or rather dark purple, while the skin is alternately red and yellow. The yellow represents the olive tint of the Mediterranean population, the red denotes the effects of sunburn. An examination of the names contained in the cartouches makes it clear that they have been derived from the memoranda made by the scribes who accompanied the army of the Pharaoh in its campaigns. Sometimes the same name is repeated twice, and not always in the same form. We may conclude, therefore, that the memoranda had not always been made by the same reporter, and that the compiler of the lists drew his materials from different sources. It is further clear that the memoranda had been noted down in the cuneiform characters of Babylonia and not in the hieroglyphs of Egypt. Thus, as we have seen, the name of Beth-el is transcribed from its Babylonian form of Bit-sa-ili, the Assyrian equivalent of the Hebrew Beth-el.

The names have been copied from the memoranda of the scribes in the order in which they

P

occurred, and without any regard to their relative importance. While, therefore, insignificant villages are often noted, the names of important cities are sometimes passed over. Descriptive epithets, moreover, like *abel* " meadow," *arets* " land," *har* " mountains," *'emeq* " valley," *'ên* " spring," are frequently treated as if they were local names, and occupy separate cartouches. We must not, consequently, expect to find in the lists any exhaustive catalogue of Palestinian towns or even of the leading cities. They mark only the lines of march taken by the army of Thothmes or by his scouts and messengers.

Besides the Canaanitish lists there are also long lists of localities conquered by the Pharaoh in Northern Syria. With these, however, we have nothing to do. It is to the places in Canaan that our attention must at present be confined. They are said to be situated in the country of the Upper Lotan, or, as another list gives it, in the country of the Fenkhu. In the time of Thothmes III. accordingly the land of the Upper Lotan and the land of the Fenkhu were synonymous terms, and alike denoted what we now call Palestine. In the word Fenkhu it is difficult not to see the origin of the Greek Phœnix or " Phœnician."

The lists begin with Kadesh on the Orontes, the head of the confederacy, the defeat of which laid Canaan at the feet of the Pharaoh. Then comes Megiddo, where the decisive battle took place, and the forces of the king of Kadesh were overthrown. Next we have Khazi, mentioned also in the Tel el-Amarna tablets, from which we learn that it was in the hill-country south of Megiddo. It may be the Gaza of 1 Chron. vii. 28 which was supplanted by Shechem in Israelitish days. Kitsuna, the Kuddasuna of the Tel el-Amarna tablets, follows : where it stood we do not know. The next name, "the Spring of Shiu," is equally impossible to identify. The sixth name, however, is Tubikhu, about which the cuneiform tablets of Tel el-Amarna have told us a good deal, and which seems to be the Tibhath of 1 Chron. xviii. 8. It was in Cœle-Syria like Kamta, the Kumidi of the tablets, which follows in one list, though its place is taken by the unknown Bami in another. After this we have the names of Tuthina (perhaps Dothan), Lebana, and Kirjath-niznau, followed by Marum or Merom the modern Meirôm, by Tamasqu or Damascus, by the Abel of Atar, and by Hamath. Aqidu, the seventeenth name, is unknown, but Mr. Tomkins is probably right in thinking that the next name, that of Shemnau, must be identified with the Shimron of Josh. xix. 15, where the Septuagint reads Symeon. That this reading is correct is shown by the fact that in the days of Josephus and the Talmud the place was called Simonias, while the modern name is Semûnieh. The tablets of Tel el-Amarna make it Samkhuna.

Six unknown names come next, the first of which is a Beeroth, or "Wells." Then we have Mesekh, "the place of unction," called Musikhuna in the Tel el-Amarna correspondence, Qana and

'Arna. Both Qana and 'Arna appear in the account of the battle before Megiddo, and must have been in the immediate neighbourhood of that city. One of the affluents of the Kishon flowed past Qana, while 'Arna was hidden in a defile. It was there that the tent of Thothmes was pitched two days before the great battle. The brook of Qana seems to have been the river Qanah of to-day, and 'Arna may be read 'Aluna.

We are now transported to the eastern bank of the Jordan, to 'Astartu in the land of Bashan, the Ashtaroth-Karnaim of Genesis, the Tel 'Ashtarah of modern geography. With 'Astartu is coupled Anau-repa, explained by Mr. Tomkins to be "On of the Rephaim" (Gen. xiv. 5). At any rate it is clearly the Raphon or Raphana of classical writers, the Er-Râfeh of to-day. Next we have Maqata, called Makhed in the First Book of Maccabees, and now known as Mukatta ; Lus or Lius, the Biblical Laish, which under its later name of Dan became the northern limit of the Israelitish kingdom ; and Hazor, the stronghold of Jabin, whose king we hear of in the Tel el-Amarna tablets. Then come Pahil or Pella, east of the Jordan, famous in the annals of early Christianity; Kennartu, the Chinneroth of the Old Testament (Josh. xi. 2, 1 Kings xv. 20), from which the Sea of Galilee took one of its names ; Shemna, the site of which is uncertain ; and Atmam, the Adami of Josh. xix. 33. These are followed by Qasuna, in which we find the Kishion of Issachar (Josh. xix. 20) ; Shanam or Shunem, now Sôlam, north of Jezreel; Mash-al, the Misheal of Scripture; and Aksap or Ekdippa on the Phœnician coast. Then after a name which cannot be identified we read those of Ta'anak, the Ta'anach of the Bible, the Ta'anuk of to-day; Ible'am, near which Ahaziah of Judah was slain by the servants of Jehu; Gantu-Asna, "the garden of Asnah"; Lot-melech, "Lot of the king"; 'Aina, "the Spring"; and 'Aak or Acre. From Acre we are taken along the coast southward to Rosh Kadesh, "the sacred headland" of Carmel, whose name follows immediately under the form of Karimna. Next we have Beer, "the Well," Shemesh-Atum, and Anakhertu. Anakhertu is the Anaharath of Josh. xix. 19, which belonged to the tribe of Issachar.

Of Shemesh-Atum we hear again in one of the inscriptions of Amenophis III. A revolt had broken out in the district of the Lebanon, and the king accordingly marched into Canaan to suppress it. Shemesh-Atum was the first city to feel the effects of his anger, and he carried away from it eighteen prisoners and thirteen oxen. The name of the town shows that it was dedicated to the Sun-god. In Hebrew it would appear as Shemesh-Edom, and an Egyptian papyrus, now at Leyden, informs us that Atum or Edom was the wife of Resheph the Canaanitish god of fire and lightning. In Shemesh-Atum or Shemesh-Edom we therefore have a compound name signifying that the Shemesh or Sun-god denoted by it was not the male divinity

of the customary worship, but the Sun-goddess
Edom. In Israelitish times the second element in
the compound seems to have been dropped; at all
events it is probable that Shemesh-Atum was the
Beth-Shemesh of the Old Testament (Josh. xix. 22),
which is mentioned along with Anaharath as in the
borders of Issachar.

After Anaharath come two unknown Ophrahs;
then Khasbu and Tasult, called Khasabu and
Tusulti in the Tel el-Amarna letters; then Negebu,
perhaps the Nekeb of Galilee (Josh. xix. 33),
Ashushkhen, Anam, and Yurza. Yurza is now
represented by the ruins of Yerza, south-eastward
of Ta'anach, and there are letters from its governor
in the Tel el-Amarna collection. Its name is
followed by those of Makhsa, Yapu or Joppa, and
"the country of Gantu" or Gath. Next we have
Luthen or Ruthen, which is possibly Lydda, Ono,
Apuqen, Suka or Socho, and Yahem. Among the
cartouches that follow we read the names of a
Migdol, of Shebtuna, the modern Shebtîn, of Naun
which reminds us of the name of Joshua's father,
and of Haditha, now Hadîtheh, five miles to the
west of Shebtîn.

The list has thus led us to the foot of Mount
Ephraim, and it is not surprising that the next
name should be that of the Har or "Mountain"
itself. This is followed by a name which is full
of interest, for it reads Joseph-el or "Joseph-god."
How the name of Joseph came to be attached in
the time of Thothmes to the mountainous region

in which "the House of Joseph" afterwards established itself is hard to explain ; we must remember, however, as has been stated in a former chapter, that according to the Chronicler (1 Chron. vii. 21, 22), already in the lifetime of Ephraim his sons were slain by the men of Gath, "because they came down to take away their cattle." [1]

Three names further on we find another compound with *el*, Har-el, "the mount of God." In Ezek. xliii. 15 Har-el is used to denote the "altar" which should stand in the temple on Mount Moriah, and Mount Moriah is itself called "the Mount of the Lord" in the Book of Genesis (xxii. 14). It may be, therefore, that in the Har-el of the Egyptian list we have the name of the mountain whereon the temple of Solomon was afterwards to be built. However this may be, the names which follow it show that we are in the neighbourhood of Jerusalem. One after the other come Lebau, Na'mana or Na'amah (Josh. xv. 41), Meromim "the heights," 'Ani "the two springs," Rehob, Ekron, Hekalim "the palaces," the Abel or "meadow" of Autar'a, the Abel, the Gantau or "gardens," the Maqerput or "tilled ground," and the 'Aina or "Spring" of Carmel, which corresponds with the Gath-Carmel

---

[1] Mr. Pinches tells me that in early Babylonian contracts of the age of Chedor-laomer he has found the name of Yasupu-ilu or Joseph-el, as well as that of Yakub-ilu or Jacob-el. The discovery is of high importance when we remember that Abraham migrated from Ur of the Chaldees, and adds another to the many debts of gratitude due to Mr. Pinches from Biblical students. See Preface for further details.

of the Tel el-Amarna tablets, the Carmel of Judah of the Old Testament. Then we have Beth-Ya, a name which reminds us of that of "Bithia, the daughter of Pharaoh," whom Mered, the descendant of Caleb, took to wife, and whose stepson was Yered, "the father of Gedor" (1 Chron. iv. 18). Beth-Ya is followed by Tapun, which was fortified by the Greeks after the death of Judas Maccabæus (1 Macc. ix. 50), by the Abel of Yertu or Yered, perhaps the district of the Jordan, by Halkal, and by Jacob-el, a name formed in the same way as that of Joseph-el. We may see in it an evidence that the memory of the patriarch was kept alive in the south of Palestine. The next two names are unknown, but they are followed by Rabatu or Rabbah of Judah, Magharatu, the Ma'arath of Josh. xv. 59, 'Emequ, "the valley" of Hebron, Sirta and Bârtu, the *Bor has-Sirah*, or "Well of Sirah" of 2 Sam. iii. 26. Then come Beth-sa-el or Beth-el in its Babylonian dress ; Beth-Anta or Beth-Anath (Josh. xv. 59), where the Babylonian goddess Anatu was worshipped; Helkath (2 Sam. ii. 16); the Spring of Qan'am ; Gibeah of Judah (2 Sam. vi. 3, 4 ; see Josh. xviii. 28) ; Zelah (Josh. xviii. 28), called Zilu by Ebed-Tob of Jerusalem ; and Zafta, the Biblical Zephath (Judges i. 17). The last three names in the catalogue—Barqna, Hum, and Aktomes—have left no traces in Scriptural or classical geography.

The geographical lists of Thothmes III. served as a model for the Pharaohs who came after him. They also adorned the walls of their temples with the names of the places they had captured in Palestine, in Northern Syria, and in the Soudan, and when a large space had to be filled the sculptor was not careful to insert in it only the names of such foreign towns as had been actually conquered. The older lists were drawn upon, and the names which had appeared in them were appropriated by the later king, sometimes in grotesquely misspelt forms. The climax of such empty claims to conquests which had never been made was reached at Kom Ombo, where Ptolemy Lathyrus, a prince who, instead of gaining fresh territory, lost what he had inherited, is credited with the subjugation of numerous nations and races, many of whom, like the Hittites, had long before vanished from the page of history. The last of the Pharaohs whose geographical list really represents his successes in Palestine was Shishak, the opponent of Rehoboam and the founder of the twenty-second dynasty. The catalogue of places engraved on the wall of the shrine he built at Karnak is a genuine and authentic record.

So too are the lists given by the kings who immediately followed Thothmes III., Amenôphis III. of the eighteenth dynasty, Seti I. and Ramses II. of the nineteenth, and Ramses III. of the twentieth. It is true that in some cases the list of one Pharaoh has been slavishly copied by another, but it is also true that these Pharaohs actually overran and subjugated the countries to which the lists belong. Of this we have independent testimony.

At one time it was the fashion to throw doubt on the alleged conquests of Ramses II. in Western Asia. This was the natural reaction from the older belief, inherited from the Greek writers of antiquity, that Ramses II. was a universal conqueror who had carried his arms into Europe, and even to the confines of the Caucasus. With the overthrow of this belief came a disbelief in his having been a conqueror at all. The disbelief was encouraged by the boastful vanity of his inscriptions, as well as by the absence in them of any details as to his later Syrian wars.

But we now know that such scepticism was over-hasty. It was like the scepticism which refused to admit that Canaan had been made an Egyptian province by Thothmes III., and which needed the testimony of the Tel el-Amarna tablets before it could be removed. As a matter of fact, Egyptian authority was re-established throughout Palestine and even on the eastern bank of the Jordan during the reign of Ramses II., and the conquests of the Pharaoh in Northern Syria were real and not imaginary. Such has been the result of the discoveries of the last three or four years.

We have no reason to doubt that the campaigns of Ramses III. in Asia were equally historical. The great confederacy of northern barbarians and Asiatic invaders which had poured down upon Egypt had been utterly annihilated; the Egyptian army was flushed with victory, and Syria, overrun as it had been by the invaders from the north, was in no position to resist a fresh attack. Moreover, the safety of Egypt required that Ramses should follow up the destruction of his assailants by carrying the war into Asia. But it is noticeable that the places he claims to have conquered, whether in Canaan or further north, lay along the lines of two high-roads, and that the names of the great towns even on these high-roads are for the most part conspicuously absent. The names, however, are practically those already enumerated by Ramses II., and they occur in the same order. But the list given by Ramses III. could not have been copied from the older list of Ramses II. for a very sufficient reason. In some instances the names as given by the earlier monarch are mis-spelt, letters having been omitted in them or wrong letters having been written in place of the right ones, while in the list of Ramses III. the same names are correctly written.

Seti I., the father of Ramses II., seems to have been too fully engaged in his wars in Northern Syria, and in securing the road along the coast of the Mediterranean, to attempt the re-conquest of Palestine. At Qurnah, however, we find the names of 'Aka or Acre, Zamith, Pella, Beth-el (Beth-sha-il), Inuam, Kimham (Jer. xli. 17), Kamdu, Tyre, Usu, Beth-Anath, and Carmel among those of the cities he had vanquished, but there is no trace of any occupation of Southern Canaan. That seems to have come later with the beginning of his son's reign.

On the walls of the Ramesseum at Thebes there

are pictures of the storming and capture of the Palestinian cities. Most of them are now destroyed, but we can still read the names of Ashkelon, of Salem or Jerusalem, of Beth-Anath and Qarbu[tu], of Dapul in the land of the Amorites, of Merom, of Damascus, and of Inuam. Elsewhere we have mention of Yurza and Socho, while at Karnak there are two geographical lists which mark two of the lines of march taken by the troops of Ramses II. The first list contains the following names: (1) the district of Salem; (2) the district of Rethpana; (3) the country of the Jordan; (4) Khilz; (5) Karhu; (6) Uru; (7) Abel; (8) Carmel; (9) the upper district of Tabara or Debir; (10) Shimshon; and (11) Erez Hadashta, "the new land." In the second list we read: (1) Rosh Kadesh, or Mount Carmel; (2) Inzat; (3) Maghar; (4) Rehuza; (5) Saabata; (6) Gaza; (7) the district of Sala'; (8) the district of Zasr; (9) Jacob-el; and (10) the land of Akrith, the Ugarit of the Tel el-Amarna tablets.

We have already seen that long before the time of Ramses II. Jerusalem was an important city and fortress, the capital of a territory of some size, known by the name of Uru-Salim, "the city of the god of peace." "The city of Salem" could easily be abbreviated into "Salem" only; and it is accordingly Salem which alone is used in the fourteenth chapter of Genesis as well as in the inscriptions of Ramses II. and Ramses III. The name of Rethpana, which follows that of Salem, is faultily written in the list of Ramses II., and it is from that of Ramses III. that we have to recover its true form. Ramses III., moreover, tells us that Rethpana was a lake, and since its name comes between those of Jerusalem and the Jordan it must represent the Dead Sea. The Canaanite form of Rethpana would be Reshpon, a derivative from the name of Resheph, the god of fire and lightning, whose name is preserved in that of the town Arsûf, and whose "children" were the sparks (Job v. 7). The name was appropriate to a region which was believed to have been smitten with a tempest of flames, and of which we are told that "the Lord rained upon Sodom and upon Gomorrah brimstone and fire."

Khilz, the fourth name in the list, is probably the Babylonian *Khalzu*, or "fortress." At all events it was the first town on the eastern side of the Jordan, and it may well therefore have guarded the ford across the river. Karhu is the Korkha of the Moabite Stone, perhaps the modern Kerak, which was the capital of Moab in the age of Ahab, and Uru is the Babylonian form of the Moabite Ar, or "city," of which we read in the Book of Numbers (xxi. 28). The land of "Moab" itself is one of the countries which Ramses claims to have subdued. The Carmel mentioned in the list is Carmel of Judah, not the more famous Carmel on the coast. As for Tabara or Debir, it will be that ancient seat of Canaanite learning and literature, called Kirjath-Sepher and Debir in the Old Testa-

ment, the site of which is unfortunately still unknown.   It must have lain, however, between
Carmel and Shimshon, "the city of the Sun-god,"
with which it is probable that the Biblical Ir-
Shemesh should be identified (Josh. xix. 41). Erez
Hadashta, "the New Land," is called Hadashah in
the Book of Joshua (xv. 37), where it is included
among the possessions of Judah.

The second list, instead of taking us through
Judah and Moab, leads us southward along the
coast from Mount Carmel. Maghar is termed by
Ramses III. "the spring of the Maghar," and is
the Magoras or river of Beyrout of classical geography. The river took its name from the *maghârat*
or "caves" past which it runs, and of which we
have already heard in the *Travels of a Mohar*.
The two next names which represent places on
the coast to the north of Gaza are quite unknown,
but Sala', which is written Selakh by Ramses III.
(from a cuneiform original), is possibly the rock-
city Sela (2 Kings xiv. 7), better known to us as
Petra. Of Jacob-el we have already had occasion
to speak.

It is in the ruined temple of Medînet Habu that
Ramses III. has recorded his victories and inscribed
the names of the peoples and cities he had overcome. We gather from the latter that his armies
had followed the roads already traversed by Ramses
II., had marched through the south of Palestine
into Moab, and had made their way along the sea-
coast into Northern Syria. One after the other

we read the names of Hir-nam or Har-nam, called
Har-Nammata in the *Mohar's Travels*, of Lebanoth,
of Beth-Anath and Qarbutu (Josh. xv. 59), of
Carmim, "the vineyards," and Shabuduna or
Shebtîn, of Mashabir (?), of Hebron and its 'Ên or
"Spring," of the "district of Libnah," of 'Aphekah
and 'Abakhi (Josh. xv. 53), of Migdal—doubtless
the Migdal-Gad of Josh. xv. 53—and Qarzak, of
Carmel of Judah and the Upper District of Debir,
of Shimshon and Erez Hadasth, of the district of
Salem or Jerusalem and the "Lake of Rethpana,"
of the Jordan, of Khilz the fortress, of Korkha
and of Uru. A second list gives us the line of
march along the shores of the Mediterranean Sea.
First we have 'Akata, perhaps Joktheel in Judah
(Josh. xv. 38), then Karka and [Zidi]puth, Abel
and the district of Sela', the district of Zasr and
Jacob-el, Rehuza, Saaba and Gaza, Rosh-Kadesh,
Inzath and the "Spring," Lui-el, which we might
also read Levi-el, Bur, "the Cistern," Kamdu,
"Qubur the great," Iha, Tur, and finally Sannur,
the Saniru of the Assyrian texts, the Shenir of the
Old Testament (Deut. iii. 9). This brings us to
Mount Hermon and the land of the Amorites, so
that it is not surprising to find after two more
names that of Hamath.

One point about this list is very noticeable.
None of the great Phœnician cities of the coast are
mentioned in it. Acre, Ekdippa, Tyre, Sidon,
and Beyrout are all conspicuous by their absence.
Even Joppa is unnamed. After Gaza we have

only descriptive epithets like "the Spring" and "the Cistern," or the names of otherwise unknown villages. With Kamdu in Cœle-Syria the catalogue of cities begins afresh.

It is plain that the northern campaign of the Pharaoh was little better than a raid. No attempt was made to capture the cities of the coast, and re-establish in them the Egyptian power. The Egyptian army passed them by without any effort to reduce them. Possibly the Philistines had already settled on the coast, and had shown themselves too strong to be meddled with ; possibly the Egyptian fleet was acting in concert with the troops on land, and Ramses cared only to lead his forces to some spot on the north Syrian coast, from whence, if necessary, the ships could convey them home. Whatever may have been the reason, the fact remains that Gaza alone of the cities of the Canaanitish coast fell into the hands of the Pharaoh. It was only in the extreme south, in what was so soon afterwards to become the territory of Judah, that he overran the country and occupied the large towns.

With the lists of Ramses III. our knowledge of the geography of Patriarchal Palestine is brought to a close. Henceforward we have to do with the Canaan of Israelitish conquest and settlement. The records of the Old Testament contain a far richer store of geographical names than we can ever hope to glean from the monuments of Egypt. But the latter show how little change after all was effected by the Israelitish conquest in the local nomenclature of the country. A few cities disappeared like Kirjath-Sepher, but on the whole not only the cities, but even the villages of pre-Israelitish Canaan survived under their old names. When we compare the names of the towns and villages of Judah enumerated in the Book of Joshua with the geographical lists of a Thothmes or a Ramses, we cannot but be struck by the coincidences between them. The occurrence of a name like Hadashah, "the New (Land)," in both cannot be the result of chance. It adds one more to the many arguments in favour of the antiquity of the Book of Joshua, or at all events of the materials of which it consists. Geography, at all events, gives no countenance to the theory which sees in the book a fabrication of later date. Even the leading cities of the Israelitish period are for the most part already the leading cities of the earlier Palestine. The future capital of David, for example, was already called Jerusalem long before the birth of Moses, and already occupied a foremost place among the kingdoms of Canaan.

Q

CHAPTER VI

CANAANITISH CULTURE AND RELIGION

WE have already learned from the annals of Thothmes III. how high was the state of civilization and culture among the merchant princes of Canaan in the age of the eighteenth Egyptian dynasty. Artistically finished vases of gold and silver, rich bronzes, furniture carved out of ebony and cedar, and inlaid with ivory and precious stones—such were some of the manufactures of the land of Palestine. Iron was excavated from its hills and wrought into armour, into chariots, and into weapons of war ; while beautifully shaped vessels of variegated glass were manufactured on the coast. The amber beads found at Lachish point to a trade with the distant Baltic, and it is possible that there may be truth after all in the old belief, that the Phœnicians obtained their tin from the isles of Britain. The mines of Cyprus, indeed, yielded abundance of copper, but, so far as we know, there were only two parts of the world from which the nations of Western Asia and the Eastern Mediterranean could have procured the vast amount of tin needed in the Bronze Age—the Malayan Peninsula and Cornwall. The Malayan Peninsula is out of the question—there are no traces of any commercial intercourse so far to the East ; and it would seem, therefore, that we must -look to Cornwall for the source of the tin. If so the trade would probably have been overland, like the amber trade from the Baltic.

Canaan was marked out by Nature to be a land of merchants. Its long line of coast fronted the semi-barbarous populations of Asia Minor, of the Ægean, and of the northern shores of Africa, while the sea furnished it with the purple dye of the murex. The country itself formed the high-road and link between the great kingdoms of the Euphrates and the Nile. It was here that the two civilizations of Babylonia and Egypt met and coalesced, and it was inevitable that the Canaanites, who possessed all the energy and adaptive quickness of a commercial race, should absorb and combine the elements of both. There was little except this combination that was original in Canaanitish art, but when once the materials were given, the people of Palestine knew how to work them up into new and graceful forms, and adapt them practically to the needs of the foreign world.

If we would realize the change brought about by this contact of Canaan with the culture of the stranger, we must turn to the rude figures carved upon the rocks in some of the valleys of Phœnicia,

Near Tyre, for example, in the Wadi el-Qana we may still see some of these primitive sculptures, in which it is difficult even to recognize the human form. Equally barbarous in style are the early seals and cylinders made in imitation of those of Babylonia. It seems at first sight impossible to believe that such grotesque and child-like beginnings should have ended in the exquisite art of the age of Thothmes III.

At that period, however, Canaan already had behind it a long civilized past. The country was filled with schools and libraries, with richly-furnished palaces, and the workshops of the artisans. The cities on the coast had their fleets partly of merchantmen, partly of warships, and an active trade was carried on with all parts of the known world. The result was that the wealth of Palestine was enormous ; the amount carried away by Thothmes is alone sufficient to prove it. Apart from the natural productions of the country—corn, wine, and oil, or the slaves which it had to furnish— immense quantities of gold, silver, and precious stones, sometimes in their native state, sometimes manufactured into artistic forms, were transported into Egypt. And in spite of this drain upon its resources, the supply seems never to have failed.

The reciprocal influence of the civilizations of Canaan and Egypt one upon the other, in the days when Canaan was an Egyptian province, is reflected in the languages of the two countries. On the one hand the Canaanite borrowed from Egypt words like *tebah* " ark," *hin* " a measure," and *ebyôn* " poor," while Canaan in return copiously enriched the vocabulary of its conquerors. As the *Travels of a Mohar* have shown us, under the nineteenth dynasty there was a mania for using Canaanitish words and phrases, similar to that which has more than once visited English society in respect to French. But before the rise of the nineteenth dynasty the Egyptian lexicon was already full of Semitic words. Frequently they denoted objects which had been imported from Syria. Thus a " chariot " was called a *merkabut*, a " waggon " being *agolta ; hurpu*, " a sword," was the Canaanitish *khereb*, just as *aspata*, " a quiver," was *ashpâh*. The Canaanitish *kinnor*, " a lyre," was similarly naturalized in Egypt, like the names of certain varieties of " Syrian bread." The Egyptian words for " incense " (*qadaruta*), " oxen " (*abiri*), and " sea " (*yum*) were taken from the same source, though it is possible that the last-mentioned word, like *qamhu*, " wheat," had been introduced from Syria in the earliest days of Egyptian history. As might have been expected, several kinds of sea-going vessels brought with them their native names from the Phœnician coast. Already in the time of the thirteenth dynasty the larger ships were termed *Kabanitu*, or " Gebalite "; we read also of " boats " called *Za*, the Canaanite *Zi*, while a transport was entitled *qauil*, the Phœnician *gol*. The same name was imported into Greek under the form of *gaulos*, and we are told that it signified "a Phœnician vessel of rounded shape."

The language of Canaan was practically that which we call Hebrew. Indeed Isaiah (xix. 18) speaks of the two dialects as identical, and the so-called Phœnician inscriptions that have been preserved to us show that the differences between them were hardly appreciable. There were differences, however; the Hebrew definite article, for instance, is not found in the Phœnician texts. But the differences are dialectal only, like the differences which the discovery of the Moabite Stone has shown to have existed between the languages of Moab and Israel.

How the Israelites came to adopt "the language of Canaan" is a question into which we cannot here enter. There have been other examples of conquerors who have abandoned the language of their forefathers and adopted that of the conquered people. And it must be remembered, on the one hand, that the ancestors of Israel had lived in Canaan, where they would have learnt the language of the country, and, on the other hand, that their original tongue was itself a Semitic form of speech, as closely related to Hebrew as French or Spanish is to Italian.

The Tel el-Amarna tablets have told us something about the lauguage of Canaan as it was spoken before the days when the Israelites entered the land. Some of the letters that were sent from Palestine contain the Canaanite equivalents of certain Babylonian words that occur in them. Like the Babylonian words, they are written in cuneiform characters, and since these denote syllables and not mere letters we know exactly how the words were pronounced. It is an advantage which is denied us by the Phœnician alphabet, whether in the inscriptions of Phœnicia or in the pages of the Old Testament, and we can thus obtain a better idea of the pronunciation of the Canaanitish language in the century before the Exodus than we can of the Hebrew language in the age of Hezekiah.

Among the words which have been handed down to us by the correspondents of the Pharaoh are *maqani* "cattle," *anay* "a ship," *sûsi* "a horse," of which the Hebrew equivalents, according to the Masoretic punctuation, are *miqneh, oni*, and *sûs*. The king of Jerusalem says *anuki*, " I," the Hebrew *anochi*, while *badiu*, the Hebrew *b'yado*, and *akharu-nu*, the Hebrew *akharono*, are stated to signify "in his hand," and "after him." "Dust" is *ghaparu*, where the guttural *gh* represents the Canaanitish *ayyin* ('); "stomach" is *batnu*, the Hebrew *beten ;* while *kilubi*, "a cage," corresponds with the Hebrew *chelûb*, which is used in the same sense by the prophet Jeremiah. Elsewhere we find *rusu*, the Hebrew *rosh*, "a head," *har* "a mountain," *samama* "heaven," and *mina* "water," in Hebrew *shâmayim* and *mayim*, which we gather from the cuneiform spelling have been wrongly punctuated by the Masoretes, as well as *khaya* "living," the Hebrew *khai*, and *makhzû*, "they have smitten him," the Hebrew *makhatsu*.

It was the use of the definite article *ha(n)* which mainly distinguished Hebrew and Phœnician or Canaanite one from the other. And we have a curious indication in the Tel el-Amarna tablets, that the same distinction prevailed between the language of the Canaanites and that of the Edomites, who, as we learn from the Old Testament, were so closely related to the Israelites. In the letter to the Pharaoh, in which mention is made of the hostilities carried on by Edom against the Egyptian territory, one of the Edomite towns referred to is called Khinianabi. Transcribed into Hebrew characters this would be 'En-han-nabi, "the Spring of the Prophet." Here, therefore, the Hebrew article makes its appearance, and that too in the very form which it has in the language of Israel. The fact is an interesting commentary on the brotherhood of Jacob and Esau.

If the language of Canaan was influenced by that of Egypt, still more was it influenced by that of Babylonia. Long before Palestine became an Egyptian province it had been a province of Babylonia. And even when it was not actually subject to Babylonian government it was under the dominion of Babylonian culture. War and trade alike forced the Chaldæan civilization upon "the land of the Amorites," and the Canaanites were not slow to take advantage of it. The cuneiform writing of Babylonia was adopted, and therewith the language of Babylonia was taught and learned in the schools and libraries which were established in imitation of those of the Babylonians. Babylonian literature was introduced into the West, and the Canaanite youth became acquainted with the history and legends, the theology and mythology of the dwellers on the Euphrates and Tigris.

Such literary contact naturally left its impress on the language of Canaan. Words which the Semites of Babylonia had borrowed from the older Sumerian population of the country were handed on to the peoples of Palestine. The "city" had been a Sumerian creation; until brought under the influence of Sumerian culture, the Semite had been contented to live in tents. Indeed in Babylonian or Assyrian—the language of the Semitic inhabitants of Babylonia and Assyria—the word which signified "tent" was adopted to express the idea of "city" when the tent had been exchanged for city-life. In Canaan, on the other hand, the Sumerian word itself was adopted in a Semitic form. *'Ir*, *'ar*, or *uru*, "city," was originally the Sumerian *eri*.

The Canaanitish *hêkâl*, "a palace," again, came from a Sumerian source. This was *ê-gal*, or "great house." But it had passed to the West through the Semitic Babylonians, who had first borrowed the compound word under the form of *êkallu*. Like the city, the palace also was unknown to the primitive Semitic nomads. It belonged to the civilization of which the Sumerians of Chaldæa, with their agglutinative language, were the pioneers.

The borrowing, however, was not altogether one-sided. Palestine enriched the literary language of Babylonia with certain words, though these do not seem to have made their way into the language of the people. Thus we find words like *bin-bini*, "grandson," and *înu*, "wine," recorded in the lexical tablets of Babylonia and Assyria. Doubtless there were writers on the banks of the Euphrates who were as anxious to exhibit their knowledge of the language of Canaan as were the Egyptian scribes of the nineteenth dynasty, though their literary works have not yet been discovered.

The adoption of the Babylonian system of writing must have worked powerfully on the side of tincturing the Canaanitish language with Babylonian words. In the age of the Tel el-Amarna tablets there is no sign that any other system was known in the West. It is true that the letters sent to the Pharaoh from Palestine were written in the Babylonian language as well as in the Babylonian script, but we have evidence that the cuneiform characters were also used for the native language of the country. M. de Clercq possesses two seal-cylinders of the same date as the Tel el-Amarna correspondence, on one of which is the cuneiform inscription—"Hadad-sum, the citizen of Sidon, the crown of the gods," while on the other is "Anniy, the son of Hadad-sum, the citizen of Sidon." On the first, Hadad-sum is represented standing with his hands uplifted before the Egyptian god Set, while behind him is the god Resheph with a helmet on his head, a shield in one hand and a battle-axe in the other. On the seal of Anniy, Set and Resheph again make their appearance, but instead of the owner of the cylinder it is the god Horus who stands between them.

When the cuneiform syllabary was superseded in Palestine by the so-called Phœnician alphabet we do not know. The introduction of the new script was due probably to the Hittite invasion, which separated the Semites of the West from the Semites of the East. The Hittite occupation of Carchemish blocked the high-road of Babylonian trade to the Mediterranean, and when the sacred city of Kadesh on the Orontes fell into Hittite hands it was inevitable that Hittite rather than Babylonian influence would henceforth prevail in Canaan. However this may be, it seems natural to suppose that the scribes of Zebulon referred to in the Song of Deborah and Barak (Judges v. 14) wrote in the letters of the Phœnician alphabet and not in the cuneiform characters of Babylonia. As long, indeed, as the old libraries remained open and accessible, with their stores of cuneiform literature, there must have been some who could read them, but they would have been rather the older inhabitants of the country than the alien conquerors from the desert. When the Moabite Stone was engraved, it is clear from the forms of the letters that the Phœnician alphabet had long been in use in the kingdom of Mesha. The resemblance of these letters to those found in the earliest of the Greek inscriptions makes it equally clear that the introduction of the alphabet into the islands of the Ægean must have taken place at no distant period from the age of the Moabite Stone. Such an introduction, however, implies that the new alphabet had already taken deep root among the merchants of Canaan, and driven out before it the cumbrous syllabary of Chaldæa. It was in this alphabet that Hiram and Solomon corresponded together, and it is probable that Moses made use of it. We may even conjecture that the Israelitish settlement in Palestine brought with it the gift of the " Phœnician " alphabet.

As we have already seen, the elements of Babylonian art were quickly absorbed by the Canaanites. The seal-cylinder was imitated, at first with but indifferent success, and such Babylonian ornamental designs as the rosette, the sacred tree, and the winged cherub were taken over and developed in a special way. At times the combination with them of designs borrowed from Egypt produced a new kind of artistic ornament.

But it was in the realm of religion that the influence of Babylonia was most powerful. Religion, especially in the ancient world, was inextricably bound up with its culture ; it was impossible to adopt the one without adopting a good deal of the other at the same time. Moreover, the Semites of Babylonia and of Canaan belonged to the same race, and that meant a community of inherited religious ideas. With both the supreme object of

worship was Baal or Bel, " the lord," who was but
the Sun-god under a variety of names. Each
locality had its own special Baal : there were, in
fact, as many Baals, or Baalim, as there were names
and attributes for the Sun-god, and to the worship-
pers in each locality the Baal adored there was the
supreme god. But the god resembled his worshipper who had been made in his image ; he was the
father and head of a family with a wife and son.
The wife, it is true, was but the colourless reflection
of the god, often indeed but the feminine Baalah,
whom the Semitic languages with their feminine
gender required to exist by the side of the mascu-
line Baal. But this was only in accordance with
the Semitic conception of woman as the lesser man,
his servant rather than his companion, his shadow
rather than his helpmeet.

The existence of an independent goddess, un-
married and possessing all the attributes of the
god, was contrary to the fundamental conceptions
of the Semitic mind. Nevertheless we find in
Canaan an Ashtoreth, whom the Greeks called
Astartê, as well as a Baal. The cuneiform inscriptions have given us an explanation of the fact.

Ashtoreth came from Babylonia. There she
was known as Istar, the evening star. She had
been one of those Sumerian goddesses who, in
accordance with the Sumerian system, which placed
the mother at the head of the family, were on an
equal footing with the gods. She lay outside the
circle of Semitic theology with its divine family,

over which the male Baal presided, and the position she occupied in later Babylonian religion was due to the fusion between the Sumerian and Semitic forms of faith, which took place when the Semites became the chief element in Babylonia. But Sumerian influence and memories were too strong to allow of any transformation either in the name or in the attributes of the goddess. She remained Istar, without any feminine suffix, and it was never forgotten that she was the evening-star.

It was otherwise in the West. There Istar became Ashtoreth with the feminine termination, and passed eventually into a Moon-goddess "with crescent horns." Ashtoreth-Karnaim, "Ashtoreth with the two horns," was already in existence in the age of Abraham. In Babylonia the Moon-god of ancient Sumerian belief had never been dethroned; but there was no Moon-god in Canaan, and accordingly the transformation of the Babylonian goddess into "the queen of the night" was a matter of little difficulty.

Once domesticated in Palestine, with her name so changed as to declare her feminine character, Ashtoreth soon tended to lose her independence. Just as there were Baalim or "Baals" by the side of Baal, so there were Astaroth or "Ashtoreths" by the side of Ashtoreth.

The Semites of Babylonia themselves had already begun the work of transformation. They too spoke of Istarât or "Istars," and used the word in the general sense of "goddesses." In Canaan, however, Ashtarôth had no such general meaning, but denoted simply the various Ashtoreths who were worshipped in different localities, and under different titles. The individual Ashtoreth of Gebal was separate from the individual Ashtoreth of Bashan, although they alike represented the same divine personality.

It is true that even in the West Istar did not always become the feminine complement of Baal. Here and there the old form of the name was preserved, without any feminine suffix. But when this was the case, the necessary result was that the female character of the deity was forgotten. Istar was conceived of as a god, and accordingly on the Moabite Stone Ashtar is identified with Chemosh, the patron-god of Mesha, just as in Southern Arabia also Atthar is a male divinity.

The worship of Ashtoreth absorbed that of the other goddesses of Canaan. Among them there was one who had once occupied a very prominent place. This was Ashêrah, the goddess of fertility, whose name is written Asirtu and Asratu in the tablets of Tel el-Amarna. Ashêrah was symbolized by a stem stripped of its branches, or an upright cone of stone, fixed in the ground, and the symbol and the goddess were at times confounded together. The symbol is mistranslated "grove" in the Authorized Version of the Old Testament, and it often stood by the side of the altar of Baal. We find it thus represented on early seals. In Palestine it was usually of wood ; but in the great temple of Paphos in Cyprus there was an ancient and revered one of stone. This, however, came to be appropriated to Ashtoreth in the days when the older Ashêrah was supplanted by the younger Ashtoreth.

We hear of other Canaanitish divinities from the monuments of Egypt. The goddess Edom, the wife of Resheph, has already been referred to. Her name is found in that of the Gittite, Obed-Edom, "the servant of Edom," in whose house the ark was kept for three months (2 Sam. vi. 10). Resheph, too, has been mentioned in an earlier page. He was the god of fire and lightning, and on the Egyptian monuments he is represented as armed with spear and helmet, and bears the titles of "great god" and "lord of heaven." Along with him we find pictures of a goddess called Kedesh and Kesh. She stands on the back of a lion, with flowers in her left hand and a serpent in her right, while on her head is the lunar disk between the horns of a cow. She may be the goddess Edom, or perhaps the solar divinity who was entitled Â in Babylonian, and whose name enters into that of an Edomite king A-rammu, who is mentioned by Sennacherib.

But, like Istar, a considerable number of the deities of Palestine were borrowed from Babylonia. In the Tel el-Amarna tablets the god of Jerusalem is identified with the warlike Sun-god of Babylonia, Nin-ip, and there was a sanctuary of the same divinity further north, in Phœnicia. Foremost among the deities whose first home was on the banks of the Euphrates were Anu and Anat, and Rimmon. Anu, whose name is written Anah in Hebrew, was the god of the sky, and he stood at the head of the Babylonian pantheon. His wife Anat was but a colourless reflection of himself, a grammatical creation of the Semitic languages. But she shared in the honours that were paid to her consort, and the divinity that resided in him was reflected upon her. Anat, like Ashtoreth, became multiplied under many forms, and the Anathoth or "Anat" signified little more than "goddesses." Between the Ashtaroth and the Anathoth the difference was but in name.

The numerous localities in Palestine which received their names from the god Rimmon are a proof of his popularity. The Babylonian Rimmon or Ramman was, strictly speaking, the god of the air, but in the West he was identified with the Sun-god Hadad, and a place near Megiddo bore the compound title of Hadad-Rimmon (Zech. xii. 11). His naturalization in Canaan seems to belong to a very early period; at all events, in Sumerian he was called Martu, "the Amorite," and seal-cylinders speak of "the Martu gods." One of these has been found in the Lebanon. The Assyrian tablets tell us that he was also known as Dadu in the West, and under this form we find him in names like El-Dad and Be-dad, or Ben-Dad.

Like Rimmon, Nebo also must have been transported to Palestine at an early epoch. Nebo "the prophet" was the interpreter of Bel-Merodach of

R

Babylon, the patron of cuneiform literature, and the god to whom the great temple of Borsippa—the modern Birs-i-Nimrud—was dedicated. Doubtless he had migrated to the West along with that literary culture over which he presided. There his name and worship were attached to many localities. It was on the summit of Mount Nebo that Moses died ; over Nebo, Isaiah prophesies, " Moab shall howl ; " and we hear of a city called " the other Nebo " in Judah (Neh. vii. 33).

Another god who had been borrowed from Babylonia by the people of Canaan was Malik "the king," a title originally of the supreme Baal. Malik is familiarly known to us in the Old Testament as Moloch, to whom the first-born were burned in the fire. At Tyre the god was termed Melech-kirjath, or " king of the city," which was contracted into Melkarth, and in the mouths of the Greeks became Makar. There is a passage in the book of the prophet Amos (v. 25, 26), upon which the Assyrian texts have thrown light. We there read : " Have ye offered unto me sacrifices and offerings in the wilderness forty years, O house of Israel ? Yet ye have borne Sikkuth your Malik and Chiun your Zelem, the star of your god, which ye made to yourselves."

Sikkuth and Chiun are the Babylonian Sakkut and Kaivan, a name given to the planet Saturn. Sakkut was a title of the god Nin-ip, and we gather from Amos that it also represented Malik "the king." Zelem, " the image," was another Babylonian

deity, and originally denoted "the image" or disk
of the sun. His name and worship were carried
into Northern Arabia, and a monument has been
discovered at Teima, the Tema of Isaiah xxi. 14,
which is dedicated to him. It would seem, from
the language of Amos, that the Babylonian god
had been adored in "the wilderness" as far back as
the days when the Israelites were encamping in it.
Nor, indeed, is this surprising : Babylonian influence
in the West belonged to an age long anterior to
that of the Exodus, and even the mountain whereon the oracles of God were revealed to the Hebrew
lawgiver was Sinai, the mountain of Sin. The
worship of Sin, the Babylonian Moon-god, must
therefore have made its way thus far into the deserts
of Arabia. Inscriptions from Southern Arabia have
already shown us that there too Sin was known and
adored.

Dagon, again, was another god who had his first
home in Babylonia. The name is of Sumerian
origin, and he was associated with Anu, the god of
the sky. Like Sin, he appears to have been worshipped at Harran ; at all events, Sargon states that
he inscribed the laws of that city "according to the
wish of Anu and Dagon." Along with Anu he
would have been brought to Canaan, and though we
first meet with his name in the Old Testament in
connection with the Philistines, it is certain that he
was already one of the deities of the country whom
the Philistine invaders adopted. One of the
Canaanitish governors in the Tel el-Amarna corre-

spondence bears the Assyrian name of Dagon-takala, "we trust in Dagon." The Phœnicians made him the god of corn in consequence of the resemblance of his name to the word which signifies "corn"; primarily, however, he would have been a god of the earth. The idea that he was a fish-god is of post-Biblical date, and due to a false etymology, which derived his name from the Hebrew *dag*, "a fish." The fish-god of Babylonia, however, whose image is sometimes engraved on seals, was a form of Ea, the god of the deep, and had no connection with Dagon.

Doubtless there were other divinities besides these whom the peoples of Canaan owed to the Babylonians. Mr. Tomkins is probably right in seeing in the name of Beth-lehem a reminiscence of the Babylonian god Lakhmu, who took part in the creation of the world, and whom a later philosophizing generation identified with Anu. But the theology of early Canaan is still but little known, and its pantheon is still in great measure a sealed book. Now and again we meet with a solitary passage in some papyrus or inscription on stone, which reveals to us for the first time the name of an otherwise unknown deity. Who, for instance, is the goddess 'Ashiti-Khaur, who is addressed, along with Kedesh, on an Egyptian monument now at Vienna, as "the mistress of heaven" and "ruler of all the gods"? The votive altars of Carthage make repeated mention of the goddess Tanit, the Peni or "Face" of Baal, whom the Greeks identified with Artemis. She must have been known in the mother-land of Phœnicia, and yet no trace of her worship there has as yet been found. There were "gods many and lords many" in primitive Palestine, and though a comprehensive faith summed them up as its Baalim and Ashtaroth they yet had individual names and titles, as well as altars and priests.

But though altars were numerous, temples were not plentiful. The chief seats of religious worship were "the high-places," level spots on the summits of hills or mountains, where altars were erected, and the worshipper was believed to be nearer the dwelling-place of the gods than he would have been in the plain below. The altar was frequently some natural boulder of rock, consecrated by holy oil, and regarded as the habitation of a god. These sacred stones were termed beth-els, *bætyli* as the Greeks wrote the word, and they form a distinguishing characteristic of Semitic faith. In later times many of them were imagined to have "come down from heaven." So deeply enrooted was this worship of stones in the Semitic nature, that even Mohammed, in spite of his iconoclastic zeal, was obliged to accommodate his creed to the worship of the Black Stone at Mekka, and the Kaaba is still one of the most venerated objects of the Mohammedan faith.

But the sacred stone was not only an object of worship or the consecrated altar of a deity, it might also take the place of a temple, and so be in very truth a beth-el, or "house of God." Thus at

Medain Salih in North-western Arabia Mr. Doughty discovered three upright stones, which an inscription informed him were the *mesged* or " mosque " of the god Aera of Bozrah.   In the great temple of Melkarth at Tyre Herodotus saw two columns, one of gold, the other of emerald, reminding us of the two pillars, Jachin and Boaz, which the Phœnician architect of Solomon erected in the porch of the temple at Jerusalem (1 Kings vii. 21). Similar columns of stone have been found in the Phœnician temple, called that of the Giants, in Gozo, one of which is still standing in its place.

While certain stones were thus regarded as the abode of deity, the high places whereon so many of them stood also received religious worship. The most prominent of the mountains of Syria were deified : Carmel became a Penu-el or " Face of God," Hermon was " the Holy One," and Mount Lebanon was a Baal.   The rivers and springs also were adored as gods, and the fish which swam in them were accounted sacred. On the Phœnician coast was a river Kadisha, "the holy," and the Canaanite maiden saw in the red marl which the river Adonis brought down from the hills the blood of the slaughtered Sun-god Tammuz.

The temple of Solomon, built as it was by Phœnician architects and workmen, will give us an idea of what a Canaanitish temple was like. In its main outlines it resembled a temple in Babylonia or Assyria.   There, too, there was an outer court and an inner sanctuary, with its *parakku* or " mercy-seat," and its ark of stone or wood, in which an inscribed tablet of stone was kept. Like the temple of Jerusalem, the Babylonian temple looked from the outside much like a rectangular box, with its four walls rising up, blank and un- adorned, to the sky. Within the open court was a " sea," supported at times on oxen of bronze, where the priests and servants of the temple performed their ablutions and the sacred vessels were washed.

The Canaanitish altar was approached by steps, and was large enough for the sacrifice of an ox. Besides the sacrifices, offerings of corn and wine, of fruit and oil were also made to the gods. The sacrifices and offerings were of two kinds, the *zau'at* or sin-offering, and the *shelem* or thank- offering. The sin-offering had to be given wholly to the god, and was accordingly termed *kalil* or "complete"; a part of the thank-offering, on the other hand, might be carried away by him who made it. Birds, moreover, might constitute a thank-offering; they were not allowed when the offering was made for sin. Such at least was the rule in the later days of Phœnician ritual, to which belong the sacrificial tariffs that have been preserved.

In these sacrificial tariffs no mention is made of human sacrifices, and, as M. Clermont-Ganneau has pointed out, the ram takes in them the place of the man. But this was the result of the milder manners of an age when the Phœnicians had been brought into close contact with the Greeks. In the older days of Canaanitish history human sacrifice had held a foremost place in the ritual of Syria. It was the sacrifice of the first-born son that was demanded in times of danger and trouble, or when the family was called upon to make a special atonement for sin. The victim was offered as a burnt sacrifice, which in Hebrew idiom was euphemistically described as passing through the fire.

Side by side with these human sacrifices were the abominations which were performed in the temples in honour of Ashtoreth. Women acted as prostitutes, and men who called themselves "dogs" foreswore their manhood. It was these sensualities practised in the name of religion which caused the iniquity of the Canaanites to become full.

It is pleasanter to turn to such fragments of Canaanitish mythology and cosmological specula-tion as have come down to us. Unfortunately most of it belongs in its present form to the late days of Greek and Roman domination, when an attempt was made to fuse the disjointed legends of the various Phœnician states into a connected whole, and to present them to Greek readers under a philosophical guise. How much, therefore, of the strange cosmogony and history of the gods recorded by Philon of Gebal really goes back to the patri-archal epoch of Palestine, and how much of it is of later growth, it is now impossible to say. In the main, however, it is of ancient date.

This is shown by the fact that a good deal of it has been borrowed directly or indirectly from Babylonia. How this could have happened has been explained by the Tel el-Amarna tablets. It was while Canaan was under the influence of Babylonian culture and Babylonian government that the myths and traditions of Babylonia made their way to the West. Among the tablets are portions of Babylonian legends, one of which has been carefully annotated by the Egyptian or Canaanite scribe. It is the story of the queen of Hades, who had been asked by the gods to a feast they had made in the heavens. Unable or unwilling to ascend to it, the goddess sent her servant the plague-demon, but with the result that Nergal was commissioned to descend to Hades and destroy its mistress. The fourteen gates of the infernal world, each with its attendant warder, were opened before him, and at last he seized the queen by the hair, dragging her to the ground, and threatening to cut off her head. But Eris-kigal, the queen of Hades, made a successful appeal for mercy ; she became the wife of Nergal, and he the lord of the tomb.

Another legend was an endeavour to account for the origin of death. Adapa or Adama, the first man, who had been created by Ea, was fishing one day in the deep sea, when he broke the wings of the south wind. The south wind flew to complain to Anu in heaven, and Anu ordered the culprit to appear before him. But Adapa was instructed by

Ea how to act. Clad in a garment of mourning, he
won the hearts of the two guardians of the gate of
heaven, the gods Tammuz and Gis-zida ("the
firmly-fixed post"), so that they pleaded for him
before Anu. Food and water were offered him,
but he refused them for fear that they might be
the food and water of death. Oil only for anoint-
ing and clothing did he accept. "Then Anu
looked upon him and raised his voice in lamenta-
tion : 'O Adapa, wherefore atest thou not, wherefore didst thou not drink ? The gift of life cannot
now be thine.'" Though "a sinful man" had been
permitted "to behold the innermost parts of
heaven and earth," he had rejected the food and
water of life, and death henceforth was the lot of
mankind.

It is curious that the commencement of this
legend, the latter portion of which has been found
at Tel el-Amarna, had been brought to the British
Museum from the ruins of the library of Nineveh
many years ago. But until the discovery of the
conclusion, its meaning and character were inde-
cipherable. The copy made for the library of
Nineveh was a late edition of the text which had
been carried from Babylonia to the banks of the
Nile eight hundred years before, and the fact
emphasizes once more the Babylonian character of
the culture and literature possessed by Palestine in
the Patriarchal Age.

We need not wonder, therefore, if it is to Babylonia that the cosmological legends and beliefs of

Phœnicia plainly point. The watery chaos out of which the world was created, the divine hierarchies, one pair of deities proceeding from another and an older pair, or the victory of Kronos over the dragon Ophioneus, are among the indications of their Babylonian origin. But far more important than these echoes of Babylonian mythology in the legendary lore of Phœnicia is the close relationship that exists between the traditions of Babylonia and the earlier chapters of Genesis. As is now well known, the Babylonian account of the Deluge agrees even in details with that which we find in the Bible, though the polytheism of Chaldæa is there replaced by an uncompromising monotheism, and there are little touches, like the substitution of an " ark " for the Babylonian " ship," which show that the narrative has been transported to Palestine. Equally Babylonian in origin is the history of the Tower of Babel, while two of the rivers of Eden are the Tigris and Euphrates, and Eden itself is the Edin or " Plain " of Babylonia.

Not so long ago it was the fashion to declare that such coincidences between Babylonian and Hebrew literature could be due only to the long sojourn of the Jews in Babylonia during the twenty years of the Exile. But we now know that the traditions and legends of Babylonia were already known in Canaan before the Israelites had entered the Promised Land. It was not needful for the Hebrew writer to go to Chaldæa in order that he might learn them ; when Moses was born they were already current both in Palestine and on the banks of the Nile. The Babylonian colouring of the early chapters of Genesis is just what archæology would teach us to expect it would have been, had the Pentateuch been of the age to which it lays claim.

Here and there indeed there are passages which must be of that age, and of none other. When in the tenth chapter of Genesis Canaan is made the brother of Cush and Mizraim, of Ethiopia and Egypt, we are carried back at once to the days when Palestine was an Egyptian province. The statement is applicable to no other age. Geographically Canaan lay outside the southern zone to which Egypt and Ethiopia belonged, except during the epoch of the eighteenth and nineteenth dynasties, when all three were alike portions of a single empire. With the fall of that empire the statement ceased to be correct or even conceivable. After the era of the Israelitish conquest Canaan and Egypt were separated one from the other, not to be again united save for a brief space towards the close of the Jewish monarchy. Palestine henceforth belonged to Asia, not to Africa, to the middle zone, that is to say, which was given over to the sons of Shem.

There is yet another passage in the same chapter of Genesis which takes us back to the Patriarchal Age of Palestine. It is the reference to Nimrod, the son of Cush, the beginning of whose kingdom was Babel and Erech, and Accad and Calneh in the land of Shinar, and who was so familiar a figure in the West that a proverb was current there concerning his prowess in the chase. Here again we are carried to a date when the Kassite kings of Babylonia held rule in Canaan, or led thither their armies, and when the Babylonians were called, as they are in the Tel el-Amarna tablets, the Kassi or sons of Cush. Nimrod himself may be the Kassite monarch Nazi-Murudas. The cuneiform texts of the period show that the names borne by the Kassite kings were strangely abbreviated by their subjects; even in Babylonia, Kasbe and Sagarta-Suria, for instance, being written for Kas-beias and Sagarakti-Suryas, the latter of which even appears as Sakti-Surias, while Nazi-Murudas itself is found under the form of Nazi-Rattas. Similarly Duri-galzu and Kurigalzu take the place of Dur-Kurigalzi. There is no reason, therefore, why Nazi-Murudas should not have been familiarly known as Na-Muruda, more especially in distant Canaan.

Indeed we can almost fix the date to which the lifetime of Nimrod must be assigned. We are told that out of his kingdom "one went forth into Assyria," and there "builded" Nineveh and Calah. The cuneiform inscriptions have informed us who this builder of Calah was. He was Shalmaneser I., who was also the restorer of Nineveh and its temples, and who is stated by Sennacherib to have reigned six hundred years before himself. Such a date would coincide with the reign of Ramses II., the Pharaoh of the Oppression, as well as with the birth-time of Moses. It represents a period when the influence of Babylonia had not yet passed away from Canaan, and when there was still intercourse between the East and the West. Ramses claims to have overcome both Assyria and Shinar, and though the Shinar he means was the Shinar of Mesopotamia and not Chaldæa, it lay within the limits of Babylonian control. The reign of Ramses II. is the latest period down to which, with our present knowledge, we can regard the old influence of Babylonia in Canaan as still continuing, and it is equally the period to which, if we are to listen to the traditional teaching of the Church, the writer of the Pentateuch belonged. The voice of archæology is thus in agreement with that of authority, and here as elsewhere true science declares herself the handmaid of the Catholic Church.

INDEX

Â (DEITY), 256
Abel (place), 153
Abel-mizraim, 201
Abiliya, 126
Abimelech, 123, 127, 128, 129
Abram (in Babylonian), 169
Achshaph or Ekdippa, 211, 219, 229
Acre (Akku), 134, 154, 155, 157, 229, 235
Adai, 142
Adami, 219, 228
Adapa or Adama, 265
Addar, 153
Adon, 131
Adoni-zedek, 75
Adullam, 212, 221
Ahitub, 154
Ahmes I., 88, 94
Aia, 207
Ajalon, 137, 142
Akizzi, 131
Akkad, 55
Alasiya, 67, 107, 157, 223
'Aluna or 'Arna, 97, 228
Amalekites, 26, 35, 40, 41, 53
Amanus, 62, 107
Amber, 85, 242
Amenôphis II., 106, 110
Amenôphis III., 111, 112, 135
Amenôphis IV. or Khu-n-Aten, 71, 86, 112 *et seq.*

Ammi, 22, 64, 206
Ammi-anshi, 63, 206
Ammi-satana, 63
Ammiya, 131
Ammon, 22, 36, 38, 64, 179
Ammunira, 124
Amon (god), 87, 99, 110, 114
Amon-apt, 128, 152
Amorites, 28, 35, 36, 38, 40, 41, 42, 43 *et seq.*, 56, 58, 65, 100, 110, 112, 119, 124 *et seq.*, 152, 160, 163, 186, 239
Amorites, god of, 257
Amraphel, 64, 66, 67
Anab, 221
Anaharath, 229
Anakim, 36, 37
Anat, 82, 232, 257
Anu, 82, 169, 257, 259, 260
Anugas or Nukhasse, 98, 102, 107, 110
Aphekah, 239
Apphadana, 111
Aqabah, Gulf of, 26, 108
Aram-Naharaim (Mitanni), 72, 85, 86, 94, 101, 103, 108, 111, 131, 138, 149, 157, 163
Ararat, 46
Argob, 23
Ariel, 213
Arioch (*see* Eri-Aku), 63, 168
Arisu, 162

S

RICHARD CLAY & SONS, LIMITED,
LONDON & BUNGAY.

For EU product safety concerns, contact us at Calle de José Abascal, 56–1°, 28003 Madrid, Spain or eugpsr@cambridge.org.

www.ingramcontent.com/pod-product-compliance
Ingram Content Group UK Ltd.
Pitfield, Milton Keynes, MK11 3LW, UK
UKHW010345140625
459647UK00010B/848